NIGHT
BIRD

NIGHT BIRD

Conversations with

FRANÇOISE SAGAN

Translated by
DAVID MACEY

Prepared by
JEAN-JACQUES PAUVERT

Clarkson N. Potter, Inc./Publishers NEW YORK
DISTRIBUTED BY CROWN PUBLISHERS, INC.

We gratefully acknowledge permission to use the following
photos in the insert:
pp. 1 top, 10, *Solange/Cazier-Charpentier;* pp. 4, 5, 6,
Wide World Photos; p. 7, © Spadem/Mediterrance Photo;
p. 8, Luc Fournol/*Jours de France;* p. 9 top, Uberto
Guidotti/*Elle;* p. 11, Sygma; pp. 12–13, © *Paris-Match;*
p. 14, A. Well; p. 15, Apesteguy/Gamma/Liaison; p. 16,
P. Paterson/Gamma/Liaison.

Library of Congress Cataloging in Publication Data
Quoirez, Françoise, 1935–
    Nightbird.
    Translation of Réponses.
    Bibliography: p.
    1. Quoirez, Françoise, 1935–   —Interviews.
2. Authors, French—20th century—Interviews.
I. Title.
PQ2633.U74Z52513   1980   843'.914   [B]   80-16009
ISBN: 0-517-542242
10 9 8 7 6 5 4 3 2 1

CONTENTS

Françoise Sagan has often stated that she will never write an autobiography in the traditional sense of the word, explaining that her life story is already familiar to her readers from the many interviews she has given in the course of her career. The basis of this book is, therefore, a selection from interviews given by Françoise Sagan between 1954 and 1980. The interviews included were selected and edited by the author herself with the assistance of her French publisher, Jean-Jacques Pauvert. In the course of the editing, alterations were made to the original texts: new questions have been introduced and the answers have been modified slightly to clarify the author's views. The "imaginary interview" that emerged from this process is probably the most accurate picture to date of Françoise Sagan's life and opinions.

David Macey

This book has been very adroitly and very intelligently perfected by an editor who is also a friend and who has managed to bring about a measure of cohesiveness and clarity to the statements I have made during twenty-five years of interviews. This was not an easy task in view of the number of foolish remarks I may have made in the interviews (either remarks that were attributed to me or remarks that I may have made voluntarily). And so I should like to pay tribute to this man, Jean-Jacques Pauvert.

Françoise Sagan

THE SAGAN LEGEND

Early in 1954 an eighteen-year-old girl called Mademoiselle Quoirez sent the manuscript of a short novel to Julliard, the Paris publisher. It was called *Bonjour Tristesse* and was signed "Françoise Sagan". The novel was published in May, together with many others. It had no special publicity. Within a year it sold one million copies in France alone. It has since been translated into twenty-five languages. Today Françoise Sagan is world famous. Famous, but not well-known. A few years after the publication of *Bonjour Tristesse*, a survey was carried out on attitudes toward famous people of the day; most of the people interviewed thought Françoise Sagan was a film star. It was probably because you were immediately caught up in a legend: money, whiskey, nightclubs, sports cars . . . the trappings of a film star rather than a writer. You wrote a book and found that you'd become a star. How does one cope with all that at twenty?

The legend was like a veil, a pretty mask. Obviously, it had a lot to do with my tastes in real life: speed, the sea, midnight, things that glitter, things that are dark, things that destroy, things that allow you to discover yourself. I'm quite convinced that the only way to understand life – or at least my life – is to wrestle with your likes and dislikes, with your anger and all the contradictions inside you. No one will ever convince me that there is any other way.

Curiously enough, you dress very quietly for someone who talks so much about the good times and going too far. The newspapers made a lot of the

11

"uniform" you wore for so long: a little black dress and a string of pearls.

The good times are something secret, something that's both sacred and sacrilegious. It doesn't always mean feathers in a nightclub. It means being with someone in the dark. As for the little black dress, that's a long time ago now. And in any case, I lost the pearls.

It's no secret that, for many years, alcohol was an almost constant companion. What were you looking for in drink?

Alcohol has always been a good friend to me, an accomplice almost. But it's also something to be shared like bread and salt. I've never used it as an escape. It's always been a way of speeding up life. But when you go too fast, you lose control on the bends because you're tired, because of your nerves and so on. Having to give up drinking was a nuisance, but no more than that.

Let's go back to 1954.

In 1954 I was faced with a choice: I could either be a shocking writer or a middle class girl. Actually, I was neither. A shocking young girl and a middle class writer might have been a more accurate description. The only solution was to do what I wanted to do – to go just that little bit farther. I've always loved going that little bit farther, going too far. And I've always enjoyed the things I've done. I've been lucky enough not to have to do things I didn't want to do.

Obviously, there are things I'd rather have avoided, like my car crash . . . things I did because I was young, because I was clumsy, things I did out of the cruelty of the young. I sometimes treated men badly, like any other girl. But I've never done anything mean or anything to be ashamed of. I think it's better to be taken in by someone than not to trust them in the first place. I'm convinced that the only moral rule is to be as good and as open as you possibly can. If you can live up to that you won't go far wrong.

I was once asked on television if I would like a daughter of mine to live the life I've led. I think that if I did have a daughter, I'd like her to meet a man when she was eighteen. She'd fall in love with him, he'd fall in love with her and they'd die hand in hand when they were eighty. You can't get much more romantic than that. The trouble is that life is so unromantic that things rarely happen that way. Life is usually far from what it should be. People get broken or something inside them snaps. I don't know if it's a question of age, tiredness, life style, or what. But there are times when things just seem to pile up and it all begins to feel like a personal affront.

I sometimes think that life is just a horrible joke. If you're the slightest bit sensitive, things constantly touch you on the raw. Little things nag at you, get on your nerves all the time. Something on television, a passing comment from a policeman or the concierge. Something inside you panics, just like a little animal, like a squirrel in a cage. So you have a drink. Some people put cotton wool in their ears, others take tranquilizers to deaden the pain. We always need something, that's the terrible thing about it all.

I think the best antidote is a sense of humor. Unless you want to end up like someone in a *nouveau roman* of course. I started to write a "modern" play with Jean Chevrier one day, just for fun. Two characters. Delphine Seyrig and Michel Bouquet. They're completely gray. They even look gray. A gray curtain rises on a gray room. He: "I'm leaving you." She: "You don't have a ticket to leave me. You don't have a bus ticket." He: "You're right. I don't have a ticket. I've never had a ticket to go anywhere." And so on. It was called *The Break-up*. There's something sadly wrong with people who don't have a sense of humor. I don't like people who take themselves too seriously. They get up my nose. Like the policeman who stopped me in the Saint-Cloud underpass one day. He came up to me snarling, "A convertible, that's just your style, isn't it?" I flew into a rage, "And a *képi*'s just your style, isn't it?" "What did you say? Say that again. Let's hear you say that in front of a witness." His partner came up and I said it again, just to be nice. I ended up in court on a charge of insulting a police officer. But I won the case. The court ruled that telling a policeman a *képi* is just his style isn't a criminal offense.

People are losing their sense of humor, their sense of fun. Good humor is becoming a thing of the past.

Are you good humored?

Personally, I always believe that things are going to work out. It's in my nature. Every time I see a film about Joan of Arc I'm convinced she'll get away with it. It's the same with Romeo and Juliet. I always think that the message will get through in time and that things will work out. It's silly; I know it won't happen. Whenever I listen to *La Traviata*, my hopes rise with the music and I keep hoping that Armand will come back in time. It's the only way to get through life, as though it were a comic opera and you already knew the ending. Hoping against hope. You don't have to hope that you'll survive, that you stand a chance or that you'll have the right to do whatever you like. You just have to use your imagination. Imagination leads to understanding. With a little imagination you can begin to understand why that swine around the corner beat his little girl to death with the poker. You may not condone it, but you begin to understand. With a little imagination you can put yourself in someone else's place and think, "He looked a bit strange this evening. Perhaps I should give him a ring."

You may have rung just in time to stop him taking an overdose of sleeping pills. It's just as likely that he was in a good mood and that your call disturbed him. So you look foolish. But I don't care about looking foolish – I'm not a fourteen-year-old any more. Being imaginative is more important than never making a fool of yourself. Imagination is the greatest virtue of all because it affects everything – the heart, the head and the mind. If you don't have imagination you're lost. But it's a virtue that's becoming increasingly rare, especially in its higher form: spontaneity. Mad, happy spontaneity.

It's twenty years since *Bonjour Tristesse* was published. What do those twenty years mean to you?

An annoying detail. It doesn't feel like twenty years, but perhaps I'm wrong. I never think of it as twenty years. Sometimes it feels like ten or even forty years but never twenty.

THE FIRST
EIGHTEEN YEARS

What about the first eighteen years? Let's talk about a girl called Françoise, who was already rich, but who was not famous and was not called Françoise Sagan.

I was born on June 21, 1935, in Carjac, a town half way between Cahors and Figeac in the Lot *departement*. My grandmother would have it that everyone in the family had to be born in the same bed. My mother, my brother, my sister and I were all born in the same bed, in the same room.

My mother's family never worked in their whole lives. They weren't rich, but they owned mills and farms, things like that. They were local squires, living off the income they got from their land. Lot is a poor area, so they didn't make a very good living. My grandfather always wore a white alpaca suit and drove a cart, but he never worked with his hands in his life. It was "out of the question".

On my father's side they were all industrialists, factory owners from the North. Their factories were always being destroyed in wars.

Did you spend your childhood in Carjac?

I was born there, but we moved around quite a lot between 1935 and 1939. My parents had been living in Paris for a long time. They still live in the same apartment on the Boulevard Malesherbes. We lived in Paris and went to my grandmother's house for a month every year. That is, the children did. My parents used to dash off to Deauville in an open sports car. My father was in industry too. He worked for a big company, some trust or other. He was making a lot of money in those days. My mother was very young when she had me. They both enjoyed having a good time and they shared a liking for Bugattis. They used to tear along . . .

It's difficult to talk about yourself. Memory plays tricks on you and you forget things. Childhood, for instance, is an image you build up. The childhood I remember is a house in the country. It was in the Vercors during the war. The Resistance was at its height and the farms were going up in flames. We were living in Lyons. My father was managing a factory in the Dauphiné. But we spent half our time in the country because I wasn't well. I was a shy little girl with a stammer. I was frightened of everything. Teachers used to terrify me. I think that must be why I never really got on at school.

Do you remember anything definite?

All I remember of my childhood in the Dauphiné are the divine evenings on the terrace, the grounds, the pond, the grass.

What about Paris? What's the first thing you can remember?

A corridor. There's a corridor that's twenty-two yards long in my parents' apartment. It's one of those strange apartments where the bedrooms are never quite right and where the reception rooms are always too big. I had a donkey with wheels and I kept trying to break the land speed record in the corridor!

Is that when you started having accidents?

I had lots of accidents when I was little. I kept falling over. I fall very easily. I'm one of those people who keep getting hurt.

Your family was quite wealthy. Did you have a happy childhood?

I remember being very happy and very spoiled. At the same time I was very lonely. I was surrounded by adults: my parents, my brother and a sister who was older than I. I was quite wrapped up in my family and I adored them all. That's left a curious mark on me. I always feel that I either began life as an adult or remained a child when I grew up. As a result, I still don't understand certain "adult" values and I don't suppose I ever will. I've never been aware of any real break between being a child and being an adult, and that's caused me a lot of embarrassment.

Of course I remember rainy days and pressing my nose to the window for hours on end. I remember feeling that no one understood me. And I still have frightening memories of the war. But I don't recall ever having felt that the people around me were cold or lacking in imagination. That's the main thing.

What about the war years, when all the farms were going up in flames?

I was four in June 1939. Everyone was in a state of

panic. My parents sent us to stay with our grandmother in the Lot. Everyone was leaving Paris, but my parents went in the opposite direction. It was madness: my mother had left her hats behind in Paris and she couldn't imagine how she would get through the war without them. Then my father went off to fight. He was a lieutenant or a captain, I forget which.

I remember him kissing me goodbye in Carjac. My brother, my sister and my mother were all in tears. We didn't realize it would all be over so quickly. My memories of the war are somewhat farcical. My father couldn't bear the idea of seeing Germans day in day out, so we moved to the Free Zone. We chose Lyons, so that my brother and my sister could go on with their education. My father was working in the Dauphiné, between Grenoble and Valence. It was a place called Saint-Marcellin, right in the middle of the Vercors. There was more trouble in that area than anywhere else in France. All that to spare the children the horrors of war! I'm afraid my father misjudged it a little. We spent four or five months a year there. The house was called "La Fusillère" because people had been shot there during the Franco-Prussian War in 1870.

What was it like in 1940?

We had a lot of trouble. Especially toward the end of the war, when the Germans really were on the rampage. Among other things, I remember being up against the wall with my hands in the air. It was all because of a so-called Resistance fighter. He turned up one day when my father was out and said to my mother, "The Germans are coming. Can I leave my

22

truck here?" "Of course you can," said my mother, quite cheerfully. We didn't think any more about it. My father came home and as we were chatting over dinner my mother said, "Oh, by the way, a young man left a truck outside". My father went out for a look. It was full of weapons. We'd have all been shot if the Germans had found it.

My father drove the truck off, left it in a field somewhere and came back on foot. He was furious, really hopping mad. Then the Germans arrived. Three of their officers had been shot in the area. They searched the house and the barn. When it was all over, the young man came back and asked for his truck, as cool as could be. This time he had my father to deal with, who was in his forties at the time, and the man got a good thrashing for his pains. You never forget things like that. Violence is always strange, something out of the ordinary when you're a child. There's something obscene about it.

No, there was never a dull moment. It was like being in a Western. I remember people hiding in our apartment in Lyons for a while. One day a German soldier came to the door. My mother let him in. I remember seeing her talking to him very politely and then fainting as soon as he'd gone. It turned out that he'd got the wrong apartment.

Then there were the air raids. Usually, we didn't bother going down to the cellar as my mother claimed it was a waste of time. But one day the bombing was so heavy that she said, "Perhaps we should, after all, for the children's sake." She'd just set her hair, I remember. So we went down to the cellar. The walls were shaking and bits of plaster were falling everywhere. Everyone was in tears. But my mother was quite calm and we played cards. We really enjoyed it. We weren't at all frightened. When we went back up to the apartment, there was a mouse in the kitchen. My mother fainted; she's terrified of mice.

What about rationing? Did you ever go hungry?

Sometimes, but not often. If by some miracle my mother found some beans on the black market, we would spend the evening sitting around the table as though we were playing lotto, with a pile of beans in front of us. It took us hours to pick them all over: "Bean . . . maggot . . . bean . . . maggot."

Did you understand what was happening?

Like everyone else, we followed the course of the war by sticking little flags into a map on the wall. I was six on June 21, 1941, the day the Germans invaded Russia. "Saved at last." Even my father realized that the German advance was finally going to be halted, and he's no strategist.

Where did you first go to school?

The first school I went to was a convent school in Lyons, the Cours Pitrat. It was wonderful. We kept being sent home because of the air raids, so we didn't do much work. Like all the other children we sang "Maréchal, nous voilà, devant toi le sauveur de la France"[1]. There was no way of avoiding that. They

24

used to give us biscuits with vitamins in them and pink sweets. I spent the rest of my time in the country because I was the anemic type. I needed steak. So did everyone else in France, come to that. That reminds me of a funny story. My father had been scouring the countryside to try to find fresh food for his little darlings and finally got a guinea-fowl from a farm. We were all sitting on the doorstep, waiting for the conquering hero to return. Very solemnly, my father opened the trunk of the car and said triumphantly, "Look what I've found." The guinea-fowl took to its wings and disappeared in the direction of Lyons. He'd tied its feet together, but not its wings. My father closed the trunk and we all went inside without saying a word. We laughed about that for the next twenty years.

So the war didn't really affect you all that much?

To be honest, I was a little young to be bothered by it. And I was very lucky. My parents looked after us well and were always in a good mood. So everything was fine really. But I should imagine they didn't let us see how worried they were. My mother had a gift for making us laugh, even when things were really bad. We used to go swimming in a pond at Saint-Marcellin. In 1944, the Americans arrived and the German planes came back to bomb the area. During one of the raids, they dive-bombed us as we were sitting by the pond drying off in the sun. There was a field, trees. We ran like rabbits with bombs bursting all around us. All my mother could say was, "Suzanne, put your clothes on. Do you hear me? You can't run around like that." In some ways she was very refined and that can be very reassuring.

What is the most frightening thing you remember about the war?

My worst memory dates from later. In 1945 I saw a film about the concentration camps. I'd been to see a Zorro film or something and there was a newsreel about the camps on first. I asked my mother if it was true. She said, "Yes, I'm afraid it is true." I had nightmares about that. There were photographs of the camps everywhere. The most horrific ones were the most popular. It was then that I decided, in a confused sort of way, I suppose, that I would never let anyone say a word against Jews or any other oppressed people.

Where were you in 1944?

I was still in the Dauphiné. One fine day, several tanned, blonde gentlemen arrived in tanks. It was a beautiful day. It was wonderful when they arrived in their tanks. Everyone was so happy. I also remember a woman whose head was shaved[2]. Saint-Marcellin was a small village. But they still had to shave someone's head. Like all children, I saw things in black and white. Right from the start, the Germans had been bad guys and the English, the Russians and the Resistance had been the good guys. When they shaved this woman's head and marched her through the streets, my mother lost her temper and started shouting, "How can you do a thing like that? You ought to be ashamed of yourselves. That's the sort of thing the Germans did. You're no better than they were!" I suddenly realized

26

that things were not as clear-cut as I thought. I began to realize that "good" is a much more ambiguous word than I'd ever imagined.

We went back to Paris much to the relief of my mother, who I think found Lyons somewhat boring. Even in peacetime, Lyons is not exactly the most exciting town in the world. Life returned to normal. My brother went to a Jesuit school. My sister had been going to art school in Lyons, so she went on studying painting. And I went to the school over the road, the Cours Louise-de-Bettignies.

I must have been nine or ten at the time and I was there for four years. Most of the teachers there were nice old ladies. We said prayers before we started our lessons. There was no way you could get out of that. Afterward, we played about. We listened if the lessons were interesting, otherwise we didn't bother. I paid attention in French, when it sounded interesting, and sometimes in history. That's all. I only listened if I felt like it. You know, a good teacher can even make math interesting and a bad teacher can make philosophy very boring.

I remember walking home, dragging my satchel behind me on a piece of string. My mother insisted that I should wear knee socks in winter. But even at that age, girls are difficult about things like that. So I would take them off in the hall and put on my ankle socks. When I came home, I put on the knee socks again so that no one would find out. I was a day pupil and I only had to cross the road to get to school – very convenient. I was something of a handful. They expelled me in the end. One day I hung a bust of Molière up in a doorway after a particularly boring French lesson. And then I

27

slapped someone when we were playing ball or something. The sort of silly thing you do at that age. I was only twelve or thirteen and I didn't dare tell my mother, so I didn't show her the note saying I was expelled. It was about three months before the holidays and I spent my days wandering around Paris. Not that I went very far; I was too frightened. Every morning I got up bright and early at eight o'clock, picked up my satchel . . . and didn't go to school.

It was lovely. It was spring. Every morning I would catch a bus to the Place de la Concorde. I went for walks and spent hours browsing in the bookstalls beside the Seine, reading and talking to the people on the barges. I joined a lending library and read Sachs, among other things, and then Cocteau, Sartre, Camus, anything I could lay my hands on. The woman who ran it kept telling me I was reading too much and that I'd make myself ill. I always sat on the same bench in the Place and caught the bus home again at the end of the day, satchel in hand, like a good little girl. Sometimes I went for walks in Le Marais. I must have walked for miles across Paris that spring.

Didn't the school send out reports?

They sent them at the end of term. My parents were surprised when no report came, but, all innocence, I said, "I don't know what's going on." We were in the middle of packing. "But everything's all right for next year?" "Of course it is." All I wanted was a nice holiday. At the beginning of term, my mother said, "Ready? Time to go back to school." So I went back to school. I couldn't go on like that for another year. Trembling like a leaf, I went to school as though nothing had happened. I got the reception I deserved. "What do you think you're doing here? You were expelled three months ago." I went home and told my father, "It seems I've been expelled." He rang the school and made a dreadful scene, but I got out of it; they wouldn't have me back.

What did you read as a child? What sort of books influenced you?

I read all sorts of things, but my early favorites were melodramatic stories. I was very struck by the story of the horse that comes back to die on its master's grave. I also remember reading Maurice Sachs' *Le Sabbat*[3] for some reason. A curious choice.

How old were you when you read that?

Twelve or thirteen. Even at that age I had a very lively mind. I was already quite widely read. I think I started reading seriously when I was twelve.

Did your parents say what you could and could not read?

They didn't bother very much. When I was four or five, I would spend hours curled up in a chair "reading" and holding the book upside down. Like a good little girl I would always go and ask my mother if I could read this or that and she would say, "Yes, you can read that if you like."

Then you started going to the Couvent des Oiseaux . . .

Yes, at the end of the summer. That lasted three months and then I was expelled because I wasn't interested in "things spiritual". I was bored stiff there. In any case, I was already more or less an atheist. I'd already read Camus and people like that. I used to go around reciting Prévert: "Our father who art in heaven, stay there and we will stay here on earth, which is sometimes so pretty." That didn't go down too well in a convent school. On my way to school for seven o'clock mass on Fridays, I used to see all the party goers, the people who'd been up all night in clubs. They were all in evening dress and waving bottles of champagne, just like the characters in Scott Fitzgerald. They were screaming with laughter and talking about what they were going to do that day . . . horse races . . . that sort of thing. I thought "Well, *they*'re having a better time of it than I am." And there I was with four hours of religious instruction ahead of me. It wasn't fair.

Which school did you go to next?

My parents were a bit annoyed when I was expelled, so they sent me to the Cours Hattemer. Then I went to two or three other convent schools, including the Sacré Coeur in Grenoble. As far as I was concerned, the Cours Hattemer was heaven on earth. Not too much work. And I enjoyed the walk: along the Boulevard Malesherbes, the Avenue de Villiers, the Rue de Constantinople, over the railway bridge and down the Rue de Londres. I used to have lunch with the rest of the gang in the Biard, the self-service restaurant or the bistro. And then I would go off home, feeling very happy.

But you did reasonably well in your baccalaureat?

I can't say I did brilliantly. I got through the two written papers, mainly because I was good at French. But the orals weren't so easy. I failed them in July. "What is the main industry of the Var?" I had no idea. And I couldn't speak a word of English. I got so angry with myself that I went through a whole pantomime act in front of the examiner, acting out *Macbeth*. I threatened her with a dagger, prowled round her chair looking sinister. I crouched down and leapt in the air, murdered Duncan – the whole works. She was astonished and frightened. She gave me three. That really was too much for my parents, who sent me off to the Basque coast for a month's holiday. Then they sent me to a crammer, the Institut Maintenon, for six weeks. I took my exams again in October.

That's when I realized how strong you can be by being weak. I hated going to the Molitor swimming pool. It was near school, but there was too much chlorine. I claimed I was allergic to it and fainted every time I went into the pool. Someone would start shouting, "Miss! Miss! Miss Quoirez has fainted! It's the chlorine: it makes her ill". "Oh my God! Get her out!" And that was that, we were free for the next hour and we could go to the café across the road. We drank Martini as though it was a deadly poison.

What were you like as a student?

31

Even in those days the Sorbonne was completely cha-
otic. There were so many people that you couldn't get
into the lecture theatres and even if you could it was so
crowded that you couldn't take notes. It was impossible.
So we spent our days hanging about with the boys and
girls on the Boulevard St. Michel, talking about God
and politics. We were all very hot-headed in those
days. Politics and philosophy, that's all we ever talked
about.

I started going to the cellar clubs in Saint Germain
when I was fifteen or sixteen. We used to go dancing in
the afternoon with boys a couple of years older than
us. The sessions were from five until seven on
Thursdays, Saturdays and Sundays. Réveilloty was at
the Vieux-Colombier in those days I think. It was marvelous. Then we would catch the bus home, terrified
of being late. We would get back at eight instead of six,
quite out of breath from running.

Did it matter very much if you were late home?

No. I wasn't afraid of my parents. They were much too
sweet. In any case, I knew nothing serious would
happen. But every extra dance meant another scolding
and I've always hated having scenes.

When I was sixteen I had to be home by midnight
or one o'clock. I had to tell my parents where I was going
and who with. On the other hand I was quite free to
choose my own friends. I was never "liberated" in that
sense. I've never been a "liberated" woman. The only
real liberation is sharing a passionate affair or not
having an affair at all. And at seventeen you tend to go
in for unhappy love affairs.

32

BONJOUR TRISTESSE

By then I was writing plays, which were quite unreadable, poems, which were even more unreadable, and short stories. I used to do the rounds of all the magazines with my far-fetched stories. They were always turned down, and rightly so. I met lots of doormen in those days. They were always very nice to me.

Then there was *Bonjour Tristesse* and that's when it all started. I was eighteen. I'd passed my baccalaureat and I'd just failed my first year exams at the Sorbonne.

Many young writers complain about their first contact with their publishers. Did you have any problems?

All girls have one thing in common: they're all liars. I'd convinced all my friends that I was writing a novel and I told so many lies that I finally had to write it. I put it away in a drawer because I didn't think it was any good. It was summer and I was in the country. The whole family was teasing me because I'd failed my exams. So I went back to join my father, who was still in Paris. I got a girl friend to type my novel for me and sent it to the publishers Julliard and Gallimard. Julliard sent me a telegram because the phone was out of order. Naturally; they always are when you need them. It read, "Contact Julliard. Urgent." I managed to contact him at two in the afternoon and got the shock of my life when he said he wanted to publish my novel. I remember having to have a large brandy, I was so surprised. I went to see him at five o'clock. He was charming. He said he really liked the book and that he hoped it wasn't autobiographical; people don't usually write a second novel if the first is based on their own life. I assured him that it wasn't, that nothing so sinister had happened to me. He was delighted and confirmed that he wanted to publish it. I was as delighted as he was when I left.

What did your family say?

When I got home and said I was a writer, my mother simply said, "I wish you'd be on time for dinner. Go and comb your hair." My father burst out laughing. I wanted to show them I was capable of doing something. But I didn't show it to them until I received the proofs. When they read them, they asked "What on earth inspired you to write that? But it's not badly written." We're a very polite family, always very nice to each other.

You say you began by writing far-fetched stories. *Bonjour Tristesse* itself isn't exactly what one would expect from someone from your background. Where did the themes come from? Things you'd read? People you'd met?

The themes came from daydreams, nostalgia, my imagination. They still do.

What can you say about your parents?

My father is one of the wittiest, funniest men I've ever known. One evening a journalist asked my father if he could kidnap his daughter for dinner. Very solemnly my father said, "You can kidnap my daughter on one condition: that you never bring her back." Then he turned to me, "Off you go, but remember: the taxi turns into a pumpkin at ten-thirty." The poor journalist didn't know where to put himself! One day my father arrived late for a dinner party, cheerfully singing, "Here I am, gallop, gallop." When he saw the look of horror on everyone's face, he did an about-face and went off, singing "Here I go, gallop, gallop."

What about your mother?

My mother is wonderful. She's a charming friend. She's kind, modest, and has a lovely sense of humor. She does a lot of entertaining. But my father is the real head of the household. They've always respected my freedom to act and think as I please. I adore my family. Losing them is the worst thing I can imagine.

You were very close to your brother. At one time, shortly after the initial success of *Bonjour Tristesse*, you shared an apartment with him. Didn't that pose any problems for you or for your friends?

It was a little difficult for our friends. We were as thick as thieves. I'd have given up any man for him and he'd have given up any woman for me. We were always so happy when we were together.

So *Bonjour Tristesse* came out. You were a success. Photographers, interviews . . .

I was terrified of the photographers and all the questions. They kept asking me to tell them anecdotes. But you can't tell anecdotes off the cuff just like that. It's not as though you were with friends or at a party. So I would say, "No, I can't think of any anecdotes." I refused to say anything. I played dumb and they decided I was sad. It wasn't true, but what else could I do in the circumstances?

Why do you think it was such a success? After all, very few books sell a million copies in France.

It was the Prix des Critiques that started it all. That was when the fun and games started. The prize made a big difference; it really helped the book take off. There was a cocktail party with lots of reporters and photographers. They were surprised to find I was so young . . . just right for stories and photographs. In general, I think literary prizes are something of a lottery, with a few exceptions of course. But they're useful for the winners. It means they can work for a year or two without having to worry about money. But apart from that, I don't think they serve a real purpose.

About that time, François Mauriac wrote an article for *Le Figaro* and described me as a " charming little monster." I was neither charming, a monster nor little, obviously. I was no different from any other girl of my age. I liked having a good time, dancing, seeing friends, listening to music, reading . . . all the things you'd expect an eighteen-year-old to be interested in.

So you really can't explain it? It was, after all, an almost unprecedented success.

It came right out of the blue. I was as surprised as everyone else. I think the publicity helped. But, there again, the book was easy to read without ever sounding condescending. And it's not as though it only caught on with the middle class. There must be some reason, but I still can't put my finger on it.

Some people say that it sold well because it was shocking and that if it had come out a few years later no one would have taken any notice of it.

Obviously, there's nothing shocking about *Bonjour Tristesse* in today's terms. It was just a story about a boy and a girl making love against a background of emotional complications. There were no moral implications as far as she was concerned. In today's terms, it would be shocking if there *were* any implications. In those days it was quite the opposite. It would all sound very dated now.

A book that sells well must touch people somewhere. In 1954, a lot of people identified themselves with characters in Sartre and Camus. And much later, someone (Jean-Pierre Faye) said that "Sagan vulgarized the novel of the absurd".

Novels were being written about the absurdity of life long before Camus and Sartre (or me). And fools have been making comments like that for centuries.

Were you really aware of having become a writer? How did you react?

I'd always believed that I would become a writer, but when it actually happened I didn't know how to react.

Success was like a huge, multicolored snowball. All I could do was stand there and let it go by. In the beginning, I found it difficult. It's not very pleasant when people point at you as though you were an object. I felt I was on display. It wasn't so much the critics and the gossip as the way people talked about me. When I won the Prix des Critiques, I suddenly had an insight into what was happening. The whole thing was crazy; I was surrounded by people and photographers and I suddenly realized, "This must be fame." For one brief moment, the spotlight was full on me and I realized, "I'm famous." The idea that I was famous only lasted a second. Strangely enough, I didn't really enjoy it. I immediately realized that being famous meant being asked questions, giving answers and side-stepping the real issues. I was too young for it. I was eighteen and I'd written a novel that was 188 pages long. I felt almost guilty, but at the same time I felt that it wasn't my fault. It was an explosion of fame.

I became a commodity, a thing, the Sagan myth, the Sagan phenomenon. I was ashamed of myself. I hung my head when I went into restaurants and I was terrified when people recognized me. I wanted to be thought of as a normal human being. I wanted people to talk normally to me. I wanted them to stop asking me if I liked noodles and silly things like that. It can be somewhat depressing to be the boring subject of a boring story. I was being trapped into a role and I couldn't get out of it. A life sentence of going to bed with sordid drunken characters who stammered out clichés and kept trying to use English phrases, people with the brains of a laboratory guinea pig. It was all part of the job, so to speak.

Everyone was convinced that I was a comic-strip heroine called Sagan. Money, whiskey, cars, that's all anyone ever talked to me about. I was getting three or four insulting letters a week. They pigeon-holed me in various ways. Some said I was a disgusting, perverted girl who spent her days – nights, rather – doing all sorts of horrible things. Others thought I was a silly little fool who didn't understand what was going on around me. Some thought I was a shameless creature who'd got someone else to write her book for her. And then there were those who thought of me as "Mad Sagan". I was very tempted to prove them all wrong, to be calm and reserved, to fight the multi-faceted monster they were projecting on to me. One day an English reporter came up with the bright idea of writing a description of what he called Françoise Sagan's "props": whiskey, a typewriter, a bottle of pills to help the digestion, the works of Marx (Karl, not Groucho) and the Aston Martin. Well, the whiskey and the typewriter were real. But I never take tablets for my digestion. I don't know very much about Marx. As for the Aston Martin, well, yes I did have one and I almost killed myself in it.

Boris Vian used to say: "We're always in disguise, so we may as well disguise ourselves properly. That way we won't have to be in disguise any more."

It took me a long time to realize that I needed a mask, that I had to hide my face. I adopted the legend as my mask and it stopped bothering me. I *did* like speed, I *did* like having a good time, even if it was all a pretense, just one more way of avoiding loneliness. It was a mask and at the same time it was me in a way. But you know

41

what lies behind masks, don't you? Nothing special, just a human being. In the circumstances, it was perfect; it meant I didn't have to make an effort anymore.

I never talked about the real me. I simply went along with the legend that had been built up around me. I told myself that everyone was surrounded by some sort of legend and that all legends were equally silly. In any case, it was preferable to being seen spending my time in the kitchen! I also realized that the danger point is when heroes begin to believe in the legends that surround them and start trying to live up to them. You should never give in. I'd have ruined it all if people had been able to say, "The girl's been quite impossible ever since she started scribbling."

And then one day I stopped caring about it all. I felt that I didn't owe anything else to the public, probably because I'd done so many silly things that I couldn't take it any more. I was finally free of the Sagan monster.

I'd seen so many people discouraged and defeated by life that I decided I ought to make an effort. It was as though it had all been handed to me on a plate. My life, the print runs, everything, it was all so unjustified. For years, I'd been making excuses and saying, "Yes, but I can't do anything about it. It's a sociological phenomenon." Finally I said, "No more excuses. That's the way it is, and that's all there is to it."

Now I'm quite indifferent to the legends that surround me. I know they're not the real me. I prefer life to legends.

In any case, after *Bonjour Tristesse* I gradually stopped being a literary starlet and became "someone who writes." At least for some people, I hope. I

42

stopped being a celebrity and became someone with a career. Picasso said "It takes a long time to become young." It took me a good ten years. I never felt that I represented the younger generation any more than Sartre or Mauriac represented the men of their generation. I simply enjoyed living the life of any girl of my age and having fun like anyone else.

Until I had my car crash, I always thought I was invulnerable. I never thought it could happen to me. It never even occurred to me that I might be ill one day. And then all at once, disaster struck.

THE ACCIDENT

It was in 1956 or 1957. The car skidded on some gravel and went sideways into a ditch. My friends were all flung clear, but I was trapped under the car when it turned over. My skull was split open. I broke both wrists, eleven ribs, a shoulder blade and damaged two vertebrae. They gave me the last rites in Creil. My brother couldn't face the idea that I might die and brought me back to Paris in an ambulance with a motorcycle escort. I don't remember anything about that. I don't even remember what happened the night before the accident. When I came to two days later, I couldn't remember a thing. It was only the second time in my life that I'd been in hospital and my first thought was that I'd had appendicitis again. The real problems began three weeks later. I had all sorts of unpleasant operations and then they tried to make me walk. My legs gave way under me. I had no control over them. It was three months before I could walk properly. I was convinced that I would be crippled for life and I was very, very frightened. Being ill is terrifying. Before the accident, I had no idea of what it could be like. No one can help you. Being in pain for a year is no joke. Chamfort used to say, "God spare me physical pain and I'll look after the moral pain." That became my motto.

What happened after the accident?

My legs gradually got better, but then I had to face the nursing home at Garches. While I was in hospital they kept giving me a new pain killer and I eventually became addicted to it. I had no reflexes left. I was like a hamstrung animal. For the first time in my life I would start to cry for no reason. They put me in a nursing home to give up the drugs. And they decided that I'd have to do it alone: every day I had to take smaller and smaller doses. It was a long, slow fight and it was quite sickening. I still think I was very brave and, for the first time in my life, I knew what self-respect meant. I discovered that I was much stronger than I'd ever imagined. It was even worse when I came out of the home. I had no more drugs and I was in terrible pain. I finally recovered after lots of hot baths, long walks and Vitamin C. I was so frightened of being a permanent invalid that I began to think of killing myself if I didn't get better.

Would you have done it?

I think so. I had the strength to put up with all the treatment, but I don't think I'd have the strength to live in a wheelchair. As soon as you begin to recover, you want to be out and about. It's only natural. But if you're not certain that you'll ever be yourself again, you begin to go mad with fear. Illness is the opposite of freedom. It makes everything impossible. You lose so many things when you're ill.

Despite that, I'd still prefer a life that has its ups and downs. A contented, uneventful life is no life at all, as far as I'm concerned. I said I thought life was a sick joke. That doesn't mean I'm a pessimist. It may be sick, but it's still a joke, it's still funny. I've no illusions about the absurdity of life, but I'm still cheerful about it. That's one way of putting it.

MONEY

What about money?

If it were up to me, I don't think I'd ever say anything about it. I've given so many interviews and when they appear, they seem to talk about nothing else. I shudder when I see the name "Sagan" in some papers. I dread to think what it must be like for the people that read them. They turn me into something I'm not. As the heroine of *La Robe Mauve de Valentine*[4] puts it, "I always end up looking as people want me to look." So I'm the woman who squanders millions, runs over old ladies in a Jaguar, takes a cynical delight in shocking people and spends her whole life in nightclubs. But that woman simply does not exist. There are passages in my books that give the lie to all that, but no one ever seems to read them.

I became rich and famous when I was eighteen. They've never forgiven me for that. Some people find it hard to take when others become famous. They always think of me in commercial rather than literary terms. I'm important in terms of publishing. But in literary terms? I don't know. I'm not sure.

A Certain Smile came out in 1956, followed by *Dans Un Mois, Dans Un An* in 1957. Didn't they improve matters?

Not at all. They sold very well too, you know. Publishing a new novel was like filling in a tax declaration. I kept hoping that people would start talking to me about literature. But all they were interested in was my bank account.

I'm still not sure if it was the money I made or the

51

money I spent that they held against me. I sometimes think people might have been less shocked if I'd bought a chain of snack bars as a form of insurance for my old age. The one thing I loathe in other people is their need for security, for a quiet life. The only way I can relax physically and intellectually is by overdoing things. I'm attracted to things that are disquieting, not reassuring. I'm not looking for security. I don't even know if I'd like it or dislike it. I don't know *what* I'd think of it, so I just don't think about it. I dislike both having money and saving money.

What does money mean to you?

In this society, money means that you can protect yourself and that you can be free. It means that you don't have to queue in the rain for a bus. You can catch a plane and go off to the sun for a few days. I've had the good fortune – and it's been real, whether I deserved it or not – to make money out of my books. Yes, it is a privilege. But I'm not ashamed of it. I *could* say that I wish that everyone could have the same privilege – I'm as sensitive as anyone else to the poverty of others – but it would sound rather facile, if not obscene, coming from me.

I'm always looking for things that are intense, but they never last. So you have to arrange things so that they do last. And that means not living in poverty. The trouble is, money weighs you down. It's a good servant and a bad master. And it has as big a hold over the rich as it has over the poor. Obviously, I don't despise money, but I don't like it either. It simply means you can be free.

Unfortunately, fewer and fewer people are interested in being free, in doing a thing for the fun of it. They only do things if there's something in it for them. And yet doing things spontaneously can be so important. France is terribly vulgar at the moment. It's as bad as it was under Louis-Philippe. Everything has been corrupted by money. There's no moral elegance left. I sometimes move in circles where there are only three topics of conversation: private life (who's sleeping with whom); politics, which means personal gains or losses ("The president's latest speech will be bad for business"); and boasting ("I made a complete fool of so and so"). It's so vulgar. That's not my background. It's not even traditional middle class society. I never heard talk like that in my parents' home.

People seem to feel safe when they have their lives mapped out in front of them. As a result, they limit themselves and reject all other possibilities. I'm not like that. When I feel I'm beginning to settle down, I panic. The feeling of being settled becomes a barrier between me and all the things that lie on the other side of the fence. I don't like falling into habits, living in the same old setting, living through the same old things. I'm always moving house – it's quite manic. The material problems of day-to-day living bore me silly. As soon as someone asks me what we should have for dinner I become flustered and then sink into gloom. Much as I enjoy handling money, keeping track of it bores me, like all day-to-day problems.

What are you living on at the moment?

At the moment I can live by my pen, thanks to my

publisher, Henri Flammarion. He "keeps" me and gives me enough to live on. I pay him back when the next book comes out. They took my checkbook away from me because I kept handing out checks left, right and center and ended up in "financial difficulties". So now someone looks after my money for me and pays for everything – the groceries, the car insurance, the house . . . When I yell, they send me a thousand francs pocket money. That's the closest I come to everyday life.

This has been true ever since I was eighteen. And in view of the ease with which I can throw money down the drain, and its essentially volatile quality, it was the best thing for me. It has allowed me to have a sort of prolonged adolescence that, as a matter of fact, I am considering quitting (which will undoubtedly enable me very soon to be a poor adult).

Don't you have any respect for money?

None at all. I hate it. Not because of the things you can do with it, but because of the way it affects relationships between people and because it ruins most people's lives. They have no time to themselves. They're trapped on all sides: money, work, family, transportation. They're brainwashed. In the subway they're surrounded by tired strangers. Then they go home to the children and the television. So much of television is pathetic and shoddy.

The greatest luxury you can have today is to be able to take your time. Society steals people's time.

Has the money changed you at all?

Obviously, the money I made from my novels changed my way of life. But I don't think it changed the way I see myself, my friends or my work.

So you weren't interested in making a fortune?

No, I didn't set out to make a fortune. It was pure chance. At eighteen I was caught up in a legend that didn't really concern me. I decided to have fun because that was what I wanted to do. But for years I've been deafened by clinking ice-cubes, crumpling metal, chattering typewriters and gossip about marriages and divorces . . . what the public calls the artistic life. For a long time it was a convenient mask. Up to a point it was true . . . I do like Ferraris, alcohol and nightclubs. I satirized the picture the newspapers painted of me in *The Heartkeeper*. I put in lots of whiskey, money, fast cars and gambling. But it was all larger than life.

Have you any idea of how much money you've made . . . and spent?

I earned fabulous amounts from my first novels. Julliard kept my money for me and I would phone him when I needed some. They would send me a check. I didn't realize just how much money I had until I left home when I was about twenty. I bought an apartment on the Rue de Grenelle and moved in with my brother. I could quite happily afford to have a whole crowd of people living off me. I could take a plane and go to Saint-Tropez for the evening. I bought cars and boats. I had lots of friends sponging on me in the nicest possible way. It was wonderful. None of it was real. I had a checkbook and the money disappeared. Nothing could have been easier. I was twenty and the money didn't seem quite real. I never counted it. I would get letters from people I didn't even know saying, "I need some money to buy a washing machine" and I would send them the money. I sent money to overworked mothers. It was so simple, it was child's play. All I had to do was sign a check. Even now, I still don't have any money sense. But when I was eighteen, I was completely indifferent to such things. It wasn't as though I'd ever been short of money either. If I'd had an impoverished childhood I might have hung on to it or been more careful, but I had a happy childhood and I didn't really know the meaning of money. Particularly as my parents were extravagant too. But it would be wrong to say I was leading a wild life. There were all sorts of stories about Saint-Tropez at the time, but in fact it was simply a happy place. Just a group of people enjoying the sun: Vadim, Christian Marquand, Annabel, me, a whole crowd of people. We were young and we didn't have a care in the world.

I squandered hundreds of millions of old francs. I don't know how I did it. It just went. I didn't buy anything. I've no sense of property. All my investments were sensational; the boats kept sinking and I was always having to buy new carpets for the flats.

I gambled a lot. At one point, I didn't have a franc in the bank and I had to mortgage the house. That hurt, especially as I had Denis, my son, to think about. I went through a great moral crisis and made them ban me from the casinos for five years. But then I started going to London, where I wasn't banned. You can't explain gambling. It's a passion, a way of life, a way of losing. I really enjoyed it.

I've had everything a human being can dream of, all the things that don't last. Now I'm controlled by a board of guardians. It's better that way.

I don't regret the so-called waste for one moment. There's only one thing I wish I had saved for. I wish I'd put money aside and invested it so that I could own a racing stable, even if it had only one horse. There's nothing better than seeing your own foal frisking in the forest at dawn and then seeing it after the race at Longchamp. Unfortunately, that would cost a fortune, so it's impossible. But I still dream of owning a race horse.

What would have happened if your books hadn't sold? Or if the next ones don't sell?

I will go on writing as long as I live. Just as I'd have gone on writing if the books hadn't sold. I don't regret a thing. I enjoyed myself for years and it's marvelous to have had years of leisure and happiness. Whatever the future may hold, I'm sure I'll never have any regrets about that part of my life.

Do you still live the way you used to?

I still like speed, but I don't let myself go so much these days. Now I have my son and other people to think about. The existence of other people has taken on a value it never had when I was eighteen. In 1960 you could still drive through Paris, but you'd have to be a masochist to do that now. Paris used to be a dimly-lit city where you drank champagne. Now it's all neon lights and Coca-Cola. The night life is not as light-hearted as it used to be. People are too tired at the end of the day to want to keep going all night.

WRITING

All I wanted to do when I started *Bonjour Tristesse* was to write, to use words. I love words. I love nine tenths of all words. Some of them are ravishingly beautiful: balcony, venetian blind, melancholy.

How do you write?

I start by writing a rough draft. There's never any plan because I like improvising. I like to feel that I'm pulling the strings of the story and that I can pull them whichever way I like. Then I work on the draft. I balance the sentences, cut out the adverbs and check the rhythm. There mustn't be a syllable or a beat missing. A writer is a sort of artisan. There's no set meter for sentences in a novel, but when you type it up or read it aloud you immediately notice if a sentence doesn't "scan" properly. I love the French language, but I don't jump a mile if I see a grammar mistake. I try to write reasonably good French, that's all. Titles are very important. A title is rather like a dress. I always choose titles I like and I usually think of them after I've finished the book.

Do you find it easy to write?

Sometimes. Sometimes I can write ten pages in an hour or two.

Do you always type?

Yes. I never write in longhand. Typing is clearer and more encouraging.

Some writers, Flaubert for instance, found it very difficult to write and struggled over every word. Some people still do.

I can understand that. Perhaps they're right. But personally I think of words as a means of expressing ideas. It's just not worth working yourself into the ground. Jewelry making is strictly for jewelers.

Do you work every day?

Not always. Sometimes I write in bursts of ten days or a fortnight at a time. In between, I think about the story, day-dream and talk about it. I ask people for their opinions. Their opinions matter a lot.

What happens if they say they don't like it?

It's a disaster. But it always feels as though there's not a lot I can do about it, once the wheels have been put in motion.

What does writing mean to you?

The pleasure of telling stories and telling myself stories. There's no way you can explain the pleasure you get out of writing. All at once you find a noun and an adjective that go together perfectly. You never know why, but two fantastic words suddenly match perfectly. It may not be what you meant to say, but it's just right. It's like walking through a beautiful landscape you don't know. It's beautiful, but it can also be humiliating if you can't write what you want to write. It's rather like dying; you feel so ashamed of yourself, ashamed of what you've written. You feel pathetic. But when it's going well, you feel like a well-oiled machine that's working perfectly. It's like watching someone run a hundred yards in ten seconds. It's a miracle; the sentences build up and your mind seems to be working automatically. It's as though you were watching yourself.

Reading *The Heartkeeper*, I get the impression that you enjoy making people laugh.

I do. I enjoy a joke myself.

Do you set out to make people laugh when you write the dialogue?

Sometimes. I hope we're talking about the same passages of dialogue.

What is the first thing you notice when you see someone?

If it's someone I don't know, I look at their build, the way they move, the way they behave. If it's someone I know, I look to see if they look well, if they look happy, if everything is all right.

You don't feel you're looking for details you'll be able to use later?

I'm not at all observant.

When you're writing, do the details simply come to you or do you suddenly realize that you've picked them up somewhere or other?

Well, for one thing, I think there are relatively few details of that kind.

But what about the scenes?

They're completely visual. They come to me as images.

I was thinking of that scene in *Aimez-Vous Brahms?* when Paule and Simon kiss for the first time. They're in a convertible and their hair is all tangled. Isn't that a memory?

No, it just came to me. That wasn't part of the visual image. At night, there's always a wind. It doesn't smell like Paris. The winter wind . . . I love that. Night is one of the things I like best. So I give the night an active role.

It sounds as though you're proud of writing "well".

Not everyone can write well. Not everyone has a passion for words, so when some people write, it's either boring, bad or just flat.

French is a marvelous language; it's always new. I find it a little facile the way people who write *nouveaux romans* expect the reader to be talented instead of the author. Real literature is always based on the talent of the author. The reader has to be enthralled, seduced. The author has to use everyday words, but in a way that only he can use them to captivate the reader. That is the strength of the author, and the source of his pleasure.

Are you happy with what you write?

I still find writing an effort and it still makes me feel very humble. I would love to be sure that I'm writing or that I've written a book I consider to be good. But I'm never sure of anything of the sort. Writing is not something to joke about. People have the wrong idea about the way I write and that makes me very angry. I can think of good books, great books, and I'd give anything to be certain that I could write one too. I believe in honesty. And, as far as I'm concerned, honesty means respecting the things you value. The value I try to respect is literature.

Do you take any notice of what the critics say?

The only critics I'm interested in are the ones who talk about my books and not about Françoise Sagan. So I'm not interested in many critics. It sometimes feels that I've spent the last twenty years surrounded by pleasant, grumbling relatives. It's always the same old story: "You're not working hard enough. You're drinking too much. You're keeping bad company. You drive too fast." You'd expect that from your family, but not from literary critics. No wonder I feel like a forty-four-year-old adolescent! The only people who actually talk to me about my books are the people who read them. They do talk about the stories and the characters.

What sort of people write to you? What do they say?

It's amazing what they come out with. I get long letters from young people and old ladies, from all sorts of people. Some of the letters are insulting. Some of them are begging letters, asking for anything between three and ten thousand francs. But most people write about themselves. They usually cheat; you can tell they're lying or leaving things out. Sometimes they identify with the characters. When *Sunlight on Cold Water* came out, I had lots of letters from women saying, "I'm in love with a young man too. I used to live with him in the country. I followed him to Paris and he dropped me like a hot brick." After *Scars on the Soul*, the letters were very different. They were much more intimate, as though people were writing to the problem page in a magazine. They were very touching. Some of them were very beautiful, all about life, death and philosophy.

Sometimes people ask what I meant, why such and such a character is like that. Sometimes they say "Your book has helped me to understand my problems." That always throws me because I hadn't even been thinking of the problems they mention.

Do you answer them?

Sometimes. I get too many letters to answer them all. And often, there's nothing I can say. Someone reads a novel and writes to tell me, "I recognized myself on page 27 – it really *is* me." It's very touching, but it's not much use to me as a writer.

Do people still recognize you in the street?

Much less than they used to. When I was eighteen, it was terrible. Everywhere I went, people would recognize me. Fortunately, it's not like that now. Some days I actually look like myself, like the photographs I mean. Other days, I look like everyone else – it depends on the night before, on how tired I feel. I think I must be shy. I walk quickly so that no one will see me. It's a matter of technique. You have to look straight ahead without catching anyone's eye. If you do, they wave, and it's all over. They come up to you and the confusion starts. "I can't actually remember where I met you. What's your name again?" "I don't know you *either*, but I did like *Aimez-Vous Brahms?*" It's terrible. If I start saying "Hello" to people I always pick on complete strangers, who stare at me as if I were mad. It leads to all sorts of comical situations, mishaps and misunderstandings.

Do you ever have doubts about yourself?

Doesn't everyone? I always have doubts about myself. If I didn't I couldn't go on writing. I think having doubts is a sign of health. Nine times out of ten, writing is a form of self-deception. Your mind is constantly hesitating between two possibilities, two extremes. The only way for a writer to make up his mind is to plunge into the possibility that is more attractive from a purely verbal, lyrical point of view. You're deliberately deceiving yourself, but you're doing so in good faith. Everyone is right and no one is right. If you're alone in front of Mallarmé's "blank sheet of paper defended by its whiteness," you can't be wrong. You don't have to justify yourself after the fact and you don't have to explain why, how or what for. You've done it and that's all there is to it. Every day I wonder, "Where am I? What should I do? I don't understand anymore." All I can say is that writing is the only way . . . to deceive yourself. But at least you do it deliberately.

Are you often criticized for always going back to the same themes?

True, two main themes come up over and over again in my books: love and loneliness. Perhaps I should say loneliness and love, because loneliness is the main theme. In a sense love always gets in the way. Basically, people are lonely and they keep trying to escape their loneliness.

People say that nothing much happens in your novels.

There aren't many major dramas, but, if you think about it, everything is dramatic. Meeting someone is dramatic. So is loving him and living with him. He means everything to you and then after three years you break up, feeling very badly cut up. It's all dramatic. I like being alone, but I'm also very fond of people. I take a great interest in the people I love. The best way to deal with life's little dramas is to laugh at yourself. It's vital to have a sense of humor, and the first step is to stop taking yourself seriously.

Nothing physically violent ever happens to your characters, apart from pleasure. The only blows are emotional blows. Why do you protect them like that?

Perhaps it's because I was smashed up in a car accident. Besides, pain is like pleasure – there's nothing you can say about it. At least I don't think so.

Which of your books do you like best and why?

It varies. So do the reasons.

You said that you used to write poems before *Bonjour Tristesse*. Did you go on writing them?

Miles of them. But they're not very good. And when it comes to poetry, "not very good" is just not good enough.

What are you planning to write next?

I'd like to write novels that are less dramatic and closer to everyday life, all the little things that go wrong. That's the direction I'd like to move in. Because that's where the real drama lies. External events are accidents. The real drama is getting up in the morning and going to bed at night. In between you fuss about or let things slide. The real drama is everyday life. You realize that from time to time, but not very often.

You're sometimes criticized for being so "pessimistic."

Yes, and for painting a so-called cynical picture of life. I can't help it. People have difficulties in relating to one another. Why should I write fairy stories? I know people have wonderful, beautiful love affairs. But they're a world in themselves; you can't write novels about them. Very few great novels end on a happy note.

Do you try to change things by writing about them?

I take things as they are. I try to describe them, not change them. I like books that describe things as they are. I like them from all points of view, morally and aesthetically. I think that truth and life are as ambiguous and as rich as any fantasy. I'm not interested in fantastic or utopian literature. Like everyone else, I loved Breton and I still like Crevel[5]. But there's nothing unreal or surreal about Crevel. I find everyday life much more frightening and violent than any fantasy. Sound and fury. Fear, exasperation, anxiety, boredom . . . anyone who is at all sensitive experiences feelings like that every single day. What interests me is the way people deal with loneliness and love. Those are the important things in people's lives. It doesn't matter if someone is a trapeze artiste or a cosmonaut. Who is her husband? Who is her love? Who is his mistress? Those are the important questions. The fascinating thing is that the psychological relationships I describe in my books are the same the whole world over. Jealousy is always the same. It doesn't matter whether you're a Parisian intellectual or a farmer from the Gironde.

You mean that emotions are universal.

Yes, they're universal. They're always the same, no matter where you go. You learn more about people by getting inside them than by running around all over the place. The only thing you learn from travelling is how to avoid the pitfalls of being a tourist. Different landscapes and different cultures don't inspire me to write.

The setting doesn't count for much. If you're writing a love story you don't need to have seen the slums. The heroes I admire are not noted for their social consciousness. My characters always belong to the same social group, largely because I'd feel embarrassed if they didn't. I've never known what it's like to be poor. I've never had problems like that. So I don't see why I should make my bread and butter out of writing about social problems I've never experienced and know nothing about. In more general terms, I don't see that the relationship between my characters and the world of work has anything to do with the story.

When Zola and Balzac write about work, it's fascinating. But I am simply not interested in writing about work. I'd never dare write about a social group I'm not familiar with. Suppose I did write about the misfortunes of someone who was very poor and unhappy and made a lot of money out of it. What would I do with the money? Build a swimming pool in the garden? It would be offensive. It doesn't bother me that all my heroes are from the same background. I'm not judging them, their background or anyone that does judge them. Perhaps that's the most genuine and spontaneous thing about me these days; my inability to pass judgment. People exist. They are what they are and I'd rather understand them than pass judgment on them. I've often been criticized for writing about characters who don't seem to be interested in what's going on in the world. I am very interested in what's happening, but I don't see that it would have changed anything if one of my heroines had started talking about the war in Vietnam. I'd have felt I was using things that shouldn't be used lightly. Of course I was against the war in Vietnam. I went on the demonstrations and signed the petitions. I'm very interested in world affairs, but I don't think I have any right to use such things to add muscle to a love story. It would seem almost ill-mannered.

What about other passions? Avarice ... ambition ...

Shall we say that some passions interest me less than others.

What strikes me most about myself, the people I know and the people I've known in the past is the constant loneliness. That's not a minor, harmless theme. It's an awareness that something deep inside you never changes even if it is difficult to talk about. It's almost biological. Given that everyone suffers from it to a greater or lesser extent, it's a basic fact of life. People are born alone and die alone. If they give up believing in love, they can always take refuge in ambition or greed. Or they can become creatures of habit. But as long as they believe in love, they go on clinging to one another.

But you seem to think that people are alone even when they're in love.

72

I do, but that's not the point. The initial reflex is always the same: I was alone, and now there are two of us. Afterward, you realize that it wasn't true. All the characters in my books are alone, even when they're in love.

What do you think of your heroes and heroines?

I like some of them, like Jolyet in *Dans Un Mois, Dans Un An*. He is basically decent. He moves fast and he doesn't stay long. And he never cheats. I usually find my characters interesting. Some critics say they're trivial. But I chose them, so they aren't trivial to me. I may have included a few caricatures in the portrait gallery, just for my own amusement. But the characters are not trivial. They usually have the same outlook as I have and I must admit that it's not too serious an outlook. I loathe serious-minded people. I think a certain frivolity is both pleasant and aesthetically pleasing. Being trivial-minded means being interested in boring things. I have no time for that. But being carefree, which is very different, is a way of life. All my heroes are the silent type. That's deliberate on my part. I don't give them much time to talk about themselves, but that doesn't mean they don't think. And I don't like writing physical descriptions of them. The reader has to imagine what they look like.

Are we meant to look for you in your novels?

Ever since *Bonjour Tristesse*, I've been accused of painting self-portraits. The heroine of *Aimez-Vous*

Brahms? was 42. I was 24 when I wrote that, but they still said it was a self-portrait. Whatever I write, they always say that. Obviously, we have things in common. But that's inevitable when a woman writes about other women. I think I share their insatiable curiosity about life. And they always have to imagine their lives in terms of someone else. There are women who have very definite ideas about themselves, who are quite prepared to say they're outspoken or even blunt. But not my heroines. They always discover themselves through someone else.

To be honest, I must be rather like that myself as I always define myself through my writing. I discover what I can and cannot do by struggling with a blank sheet of paper. When I'm not writing, I always see myself in terms of someone else. Besides, anyone who writes novels is a liar. *Remembrance of Things Past* is one of the novels I admire most, but it's the work of a complete liar. Everything in it has been changed and transformed. It's one of the most beautiful, truthful books in the world, precisely because Proust accepted that he was constantly lying. If a writer ever achieves a balance between what he is and what he says, he ceases to be a writer. A writer is a compulsive liar, a dreamer, a mythomaniac or a madman. There is no such thing as a well-balanced writer.

How would you define literature?

I see literature as a form of madness. You invent characters who become your friends and you end up knowing them better than you know your own parents. All this deliberately "modern" writing bores me.

I don't believe in techniques and all this talk about a revival of the novel. We have the whole human being to explore. A writer is like a woodcutter. The tree is quite big enough and he doesn't have to be testing the edge of his axe all the time.

Literature used to mean Balzac with his dressing gown and his cup of coffee, writing "He saw her and fell madly in love with her. She died weeping at his feet, one last tear flowing down her cheek." Then there was Proust, and Dostoevsky describing Prince Myshkin's epileptic fits. Every writer dreams of being Proust. But Proust was a genius.

Are you?

I think I have talent, but I'm no genius.

Do you read a lot?

When I was fifteen I would read anything I could lay my hands on. It was like a reflex. Words, words, words, as Sartre would say. I once spent four months in a mountain chalet near Grenoble. I was tired and ill; I was anemic. I read a lot during those four months: Nietzsche, Gide, Sartre, Dostoevsky, in fact the Russians in general. A lot of poetry, Shakespeare, Benjamin Constant. That was while the Resistance was active in the Vercors. Then I discovered Stendhal and some of Faulkner's novels. In that area, I have very classical taste. I admire the talent of a lot of contemporary writers; Simone de Beauvoir, especially *She Came to Stay;* Nathalie Sarraute's early novels; some things by Françoise Mallet-Joris, Yves Navarre,

Malraux. But the only one who has never let me down is Sartre. His characters are there in front of you. They take shape as you read about their lives.

What is the first thing that strikes you about a writer?

The "voice". Some writers have a voice. It's like someone talking to you. You can hear it from the first line. That's what counts, the voice or the tone.

What do you read most often?

I often reread Proust. I remember reading him in India. Now I always associate Madame Verdurin's *salon* with the waters of the Ganges, which is strange. I often read Sartre. And Racine, even though I found him boring when I was at school. But once you begin to love the French language, you begin to be fascinated by Racine. Then I know lots of poems by heart; I can recite Eluard and Apollinaire by the yard.

Have you ever reread *Bonjour Tristesse*?

No, never. I did flip through it a long time ago. I noticed things I'd never even seen at the time. Some of them were naive, others were clever.

Do you read American writers?

Yes, I have read Norman Mailer, William Styron, Joseph Heller, Faulkner, Saul Bellow, Fitzgerald, etc.

I admire Styron greatly, especially *Lie Down in Dark-ness.* I like Saul Bellow very much, notably *Humboldt's Gift.* What I cannot understand is the apparent indifference of Americans to Tennessee Williams, whom, like three-quarters of the young people in France – and older people as well – I consider a very great poet and a marvelous writer.

Do you consider yourself to have been influenced by the Existentialists?

I have admired Sartre ever since I was fifteen years old. It began with *Reflections on the Jewish Question,* and my admiration has never since diminished or been in doubt. I liked *The Paths of Liberty* a great deal, even though he himself told me he was not enthusiastic about it, and especially, more recently, *Words,* one of the most brilliant books I have ever read in my entire life. With Sartre, things are different: I love his books and I loved the man. The books, because they are highly intelligent and entirely honest; the man, because he may be the only famous man I have ever known who was completely contemptuous of honors and money and, above all, had not the least pretension about himself, either privately or as a public personality.

I do not know to what extent his books have influenced me – one never knows – but the major theme of his writings and the basis of his morality, that one is what one does and not what one is supposed to be, appears to me to be one of the strongest and most uncompromising elements in morality as I understand it, as it applies to one's relations to others. My way of looking at life, in effect, is influenced more by the people I have loved than by the people I have read. As for Camus, I am much less impressed by him, even though I perceive him to be a completely honest man. If I were forced to select a mentor, I would name Jean-Paul Sartre.

THEATRE AND FILMS

When and why did you begin writing for the stage?

I first thought of writing for the stage in 1954. Florence Malraux, Bernard Frank and I went to François Michel's place in Montaplan. It was a huge, lonely house on a hill. It was dark and several stories high; it looked rather like a bunker. Bernard Frank told us a story about a young braggart who, in certain circumstances, became a complete coward, a trembling lover. It made a big impact on me. I didn't write my first play until the winter of 1957. I'd just finished *Dans Un Mois, Dans Un An*. I was staying with friends in a windmill near Milly-La-Forêt. It was cold, the evenings were long and I was rather bored. To pass the time, I started writing a story about some people who were shut up in a castle. I didn't think of it as a play at the time. I don't think it even had a title. Shortly after that, Jacques Brenner asked me for something for his *Cahiers des Saisons*. I showed him the outline of a play: *Château en Suède*. André Barsacq read it. He was never very talkative, but he told me he liked the tone. He asked me to rewrite it. It wasn't long enough and it had no backbone to it. It wasn't clear enough and the jokes wouldn't work on stage. When you're writing for the stage you have to tie knots and then untie them. Barsacq was a great help. For a month we met every other day and worked on the play until it was just right. So my beginnings as a dramatist are all due to chance.

The reason I've gone on writing plays may be less valid, but it's a very real reason: I enjoy the rehearsals. You're in Paris, hanging around the theatre. It's like a huge family. Even the smell of an empty theatre fascinates me, the smell of the theatre when people start work. It's fantastic to hear people "saying" the words you've written, at least at the beginning. It's wonderful. It's right and it's not quite right. You recognize the words, but at the same time you don't quite recognize them. Suddenly, it all falls into place. An actor speaks the line just the way you want it to be spoken and suddenly your characters are real to you. I love standing in the wings during rehearsals. It's like a game, the way the actors come up to you and ask, very seriously, "What am I thinking of when I open the door?", the way they express things you never even thought of when you wrote the dialogue.

Putting on a play is like playing with toy bricks. I like the atmosphere of the rehearsals, being in contact with other people, the squabbles between the actors, the scene-shifters and the director. You spend a month and a half with other people, and then you probably never see them again. I never set foot in the theatre after the first night. A first night is always amazing. Everyone's teeth are chattering. It's half farce and half bullfight. Dress rehearsals are so melodramatic. Even the prompter is in tears and hugs you. In the middle of all the excitement you suddenly realize how much is at stake for everyone and you begin to feel dizzy. I often get stage-fright when I see an actor looking as pale as death. I really want the play to go well for his sake. I'm not being altruistic; it's just that I can see that he's in a worse panic than I am! When a play doesn't go well I feel sorry for the actors. I feel as if I'm wasting their time and their talent.

Do you write with specific actors in mind?

I did once. I wrote a play for Marie Bell. I know how she behaves, the way she stalks around like a lioness, the way she talks. I really enjoyed writing lines that she might well have come out with in real life.

Many dramatists are very annoyed if they get bad notices. Are you like that?

Unlike many dramatists, I'm not very upset by bad notices. Partly because putting on a play is always a gamble and I'm a good loser. It must be terrifying to be a critic, assuming you're honest about the job – and most critics are – so it's all part of the game. So far, I've averaged one success in two. The most exciting thing of all is the complete uncertainty as to the reception my next play will get.

Do you see any difference between your novels and your plays?

People have sometimes pointed out that the difference is that the plays are very traditional. That's deliberate. I like the old-fashioned side to them. Besides, the theatre is out of date. All these theories about a new theatre seem very woolly to me. The theatre is the classic middle class art form because it costs at least twenty francs to go to the theatre. Unless you go to the so-called experimental theatres where they force people who are worn out at the end of a day's work to watch Brecht and Pirandello. I find that incredibly snobbish. Just because the tickets cost only five francs they think they can make people sit through plays that are good for them, that they have the right to educate people.

People go to work all day, they travel long distances and then they have to go to the theatre to be educated. What gives anyone the right to educate the working class? As if the working class couldn't educate itself! These so-called left wing intellectuals must really despise what they call the working class. What right do they have to drag people into their theatres like that? It's so vulgar. They should put on Feydeau to entertain people, to help them relax, just like the people who pay sixty francs to see Barillet and Grédy or even my plays. The only way to develop an art form is to let everyone do what he likes. Everyone should be able to follow their own bent without trying to impose their views on other people. For me, the theatre is primarily a form of entertainment. Even if there is such a thing as committed, political theatre, it's still a form of entertainment. I can't stand the way the experimental groups talk about the working class. There is no such thing as the working class. They are just ordinary people. They're the same age as theatre people. They have the same sexual needs and the same sensitivity. The only difference is that they're poor. But there is no such thing as the working class. Brecht, Pirandello and Sartre can be marvelous on stage. But so can Labiche, Feydeau and Anouilh.

I don't think of myself as writing light comedy for the boulevard theatres. There are no special effects in my plays and even if they are performed on the boulevards, I still say that I don't write light comedies. Ever since the time of the Greeks, the theatre has been a form of entertainment.

Didn't you once direct a play?

Yes, partly out of curiosity, partly to annoy the specialists. It was *Bonjour, Impair, et Passe*. I soon found out that being a director is a craft in itself and that I'm not cut out for it. It was a disaster. You have to know the ropes, but above all you have to have the authority to make people work. I picked personal friends: Trintignant, Juliette Gréco and Michel de Ré. Everyone kept saying, "That's enough work for one day. Let's go for a drink." And off we went. All I should do is make notes during the rehearsals and give them to the director.

I've also dabbled in films. I'd had enough of seeing my books being turned into idiotic films. The only film version I liked was *Aimez-Vous Brahms?* The worst was the film version of *A Certain Smile*. So I decided to work on the screen version of *La Chamade* myself. The Hakim brothers wanted to film it with Bardot and Belmondo. I knew Bardot wanted the part, but I didn't really see her in that role. And if the Hakim brothers had bought the rights, I'd have had absolutely no control over the film. So I decided it would be better to work with Alain Cavalier. I didn't know him very well, but the way he saw the book and the characters was very similar to the way I saw them. I'd seen his earlier films and liked them. Besides, it's always fun to go back to characters you've half forgotten and bring them to life again. The film is very close to the book, which is the way Alain wanted it to be. Then I made *Landru* with Claude Chabrol. I liked Chabrol and I once wrote a very good review of one of his films when I was working as a critic for *L'Express*. Beauregard asked me to make a film with him. We wrote the screenplay in less than a week. It was great fun. But films are still just a sideline. I write novels because that's my vocation and I write plays because I enjoy it.

What do you enjoy so much about the theatre?

It's a kind of madness. You write a play, then you work on it for months during rehearsals. Then one evening the moment of truth arrives. You sit in a box with a few friends, like a boxer with his seconds and you watch your play. It's either a hit or a flop and you can't do anything about it. Afterward, it loses a lot of its interest. A play is a game you rapidly lose control of. It escapes from you, just like the characters.

Actually, writing a play is great fun. It goes very quickly, like an intellectual version of ping-pong. An idea, or the basis for a plot comes to me. I start from that and then think about the characters. Then I write very quickly. The only changes I make are made during rehearsals. It all depends on the actors. If a line doesn't sound right on stage, it has to be changed. You often have to add extra dialogue to give the actors time to change in the wings or for technical reasons.

Writing plays and novels are two very different things. Plays are easier because they're so much more extrovert, whereas you become much more involved with a novel. In a play you have to explain things and cross the T's and dot the I's. In a novel you can simply suggest things. You have much less freedom in a play, as there are definite rules as to time and place. All you have is a few characters talking to each other on a stage. In a novel you have much greater freedom. You can spend as many pages as you like describing a river or a door knob. Paradoxically enough, it's easier to write for the stage, precisely because there are rules. If you get stuck, you can follow the rules. That makes the dramatist's job much easier. The important thing is that there has to be a logical development. There is a dramatic progression toward the end and you have to follow certain pathways to get there. It's like squash: it doesn't matter if you hit the ball to the left or to the right, it always comes back to the middle of the court. When you're writing a novel, there are no walls and the ball may go out of the window. You may never find it again. I find the freedom of the novel frightening. Obviously, I start out with a basic theme or idea, but there's no set plan. I move from one detail to the next, always bringing out the same theme. You can't do that in a play. In a novel, I need three or four characters. I plunge into it. I huff and I puff because I can't say what I want to say. I make mistakes and I get confused. But the plays are written very quickly, with very little difficulty. It's like being a carpenter: you put beams and planks together, then you can make the characters come and go as you wish.

So you're a novelist who writes plays for fun.

I enjoy the theatre, but the novel is my first love. As I said, I love the rehearsals, the atmosphere of the theatre itself, the actors. I like talking to them. But I have a passion for literature, because you have to be alone to write.

PEOPLE

You said that you were quite incapable of passing judgment on anyone.

Human beings may be only flesh and blood, but they are quite extraordinary creatures. Even if someone does something truly horrible, there is always a reason, some weakness which meant that he couldn't do anything else. I don't think that I could ever cast the first stone. I could never find anyone guilty. I love people too much to be able to bring myself to hurt them. And you do hurt people when you judge them.

Even people you love?

Loving doesn't just mean being in love. It's really a question of understanding and understanding means that there are things you don't have to talk about, things that you can simply pass over.

What makes a life . . . a human life?

What does that mean . . . "a life . . . a human life"? They're just words. I believe that people have permanent instincts, wants and needs. Nothing can change that. People need to feel safe, to be warm and to be loved. I see that every day. Every day I see that people need somewhere to sleep, someone to tell them they love them. They don't want to be alone or afraid. They don't want to wake up in a cold sweat. People are afraid of life, afraid of going short. They really are afraid. But there is something magnificent in everyone; no one is born completely ugly. Sometimes they never find that something, because no one has ever looked for it. Then things turn out badly and people end up in court.

The trouble is that people are never quite what they seem to be at first sight, which is worrying. I'm fatally attracted to things that are disturbing, things that unsettle a way of life. The moment it looks as though someone might fall and hurt himself, I become interested in him.

Aren't you looking for an image of yourself in other people?

I don't need a mirror. When I look at someone I want to see that person. I'm not looking at my reflection in his eyes.

What is happiness?

If you believe everything you read in the newspapers, the happiness most people are looking for is a mixture of television, weekends away and car crashes. That's a rather summary judgment. People are more refined, sensitive and lonely than one usually thinks. A washing machine never made any woman happy. Nor did being photographed at a dance for a glossy magazine.

Deep down inside people are worried. Whenever I publish a new book, I get letters saying, "I've been through that too; I've seen things like that; I've suffered like that." These days, being worried is as normal as having teeth and hair. What do you expect? People lead colorless lives: they have no choice. I'm very lucky because I can do what I like. I can even live alone if I like. But most people lead terrible lives. They're grabbed by the scruff of the neck and made to work from morning to night. In the evening, they watch stupid television programs. They're never alone. They're always trapped by other people. They never have a moment to themselves just to listen to time ticking away. For most people, life is just one mad merry-go-round.

But I love people. I feel that the things they do, the way they behave affect me directly. If someone acts like a beast, that affects me. If someone is good and intelligent, that concerns me too. I think that's very important. If I know that someone is generous and then see her behaving as though she were mean, it's the generosity I remember. Even horrible people can have something about them. If they have, I forget how horrible they are. I trust people.

I don't know if I'm getting old or if it's just other people, but they seem to be less happy and less frightened than they used to be. I remember when I lived with my brother. We always used to say, "Let's all enjoy ourselves and have a good time. After all, they'll soon be dropping atom bombs on us." People don't believe that any more. They believe in being worn down, but they no longer believe in death. They're right, but it's much less romantic that way and it doesn't make you want to speed things up.

What sort of people do you like?

It may sound a little silly, but I like people who behave naturally, who don't try to be something they're not. By that, I mean people who are kind and understanding and who have a sort of inner happiness. I

93

really love kind people.

I also like people who sprawl in armchairs and stretch out in bed, quiet, alone, relaxed and happy to be that way. I like people who retain their self control in public and don't care what others might think.

What sort of people do you dislike?

I loathe people who are intolerant and who always think they are in the right. Noisy, self-satisfied people. Stupid people bore me. I really cannot stand that mixture of self-confidence and mediocrity. That bores me to death. I dislike false martyrs, pseudo-intellectuals and people who talk too much. Respect for money, hypocrisy, clichés and middle class common sense all get on my nerves. You can't do without common sense, but I hate people who make a fetish of it.

Are you afraid of anyone?

People who are never afraid to look life in the eye frighten me. Deep inside me, I envy people who are sure of themselves. I never feel sure of myself.

What about the rich?

Rich people bore me. They're rich because they hold on to their money and that means they're always saying no to other people. I've often noticed that it's always the rich that talk about money. There's something different about them; they lead safe, sheltered lives, so they develop different reflexes. They may well be as intelligent, as gifted and as sensitive as anyone else and they're not a race apart. But my friends, the people I love because they're still natural and trusting, are far from rich and never talk about money. Friends . . . that's a very important word. The people I love are the most important thing in the world. I feel at my best when I'm with them because they love me for what I am. There aren't many of them.

Who are they?

The people I live with, the people who are around me. We talk for hours on end about all sorts of things. We never stop talking.

Do all your friends come from the same background? Haven't you ever met a fascinating plumber or an attractive gamekeeper?

Of course I have.

But you never talk about them in your novels. You say that you can only write about things you know. What exactly is the Sagan clique?

There's been a lot of talk about the Sagan clique. But there is no clique and there never has been. I have friends, that's all. I've known some of them for twenty years or more. They aren't my courtiers. In fact they often treat me quite badly. They say things like, "Oh, I see you've written another little novel." Sometimes I think I'd rather be surrounded by people who flattered me and showered me with flowers. It would make a nice change.

What do you look for in your friends?

I look for two qualities in my friends: they must have a sense of humor and they mustn't be selfish. Those qualities are the two things that any friendship needs. People with a sense of humor are intelligent but not pretentious. People who are unselfish are kind and generous. I used to be very thoughtless and hurtful to the people around me, but I'm more careful now. I don't claim never to hurt them, but I am more careful than I used to be. They've often helped to shield me from my own emotions. If you've been having an affair with the same man for a long time, you begin to want to freewheel.

Do your friends take advantage of you, as people claim?

Everyone says that people are constantly sponging on me. It's not true, but even if it were true I wouldn't care. I'm lazy enough to understand other people's laziness. A spare bank note is just like St. Martin's cloak. The only thing to do with it is to tear it in two. What I find much more difficult is moral sponging. Having to talk to people, having to listen to them, being a one-woman Salvation Army. There are days when I feel like listening. But there are also days when I simply cannot stand it. It's true that I like people who are lost, people who don't know where they are. I feel that I can help them. The best way to help people like that is to listen to them. I've always looked after friends who came to cry on my shoulder. Friends or

The house in Carjac
where Françoise, her
mother, brother and sister
were born.

The three Quoirez children.
From left to right:
Suzanne, Françoise,
Jacques.

*Françoise's parents, Marie
and Pierre Quoirez.*

Françoise, age 6.

Françoise and an American soldier during the liberation of France.

On horseback at her uncle's farm in the Lot.

acing page:
ublicity shot for
onjour Tristesse.

ix months after her car
rash. With Jean Seberg,
ar of the movie Bonjour Tristesse, *on the*
rench Riviera in August 1957.

In a Havana pub in 1960 with
brother Jacques. Françoise
was covering the
revolution for L'Express

*With Massimo Gargia
in Saint Tropez.*

Facing page and above:
Françoise with her son Denis.

*Bob Westhoff, Denis's
father, Sagan's second husband.*

The Lotus Seven.

Facing page:
Directing her first film,
The Blue Ferns, *1975.*

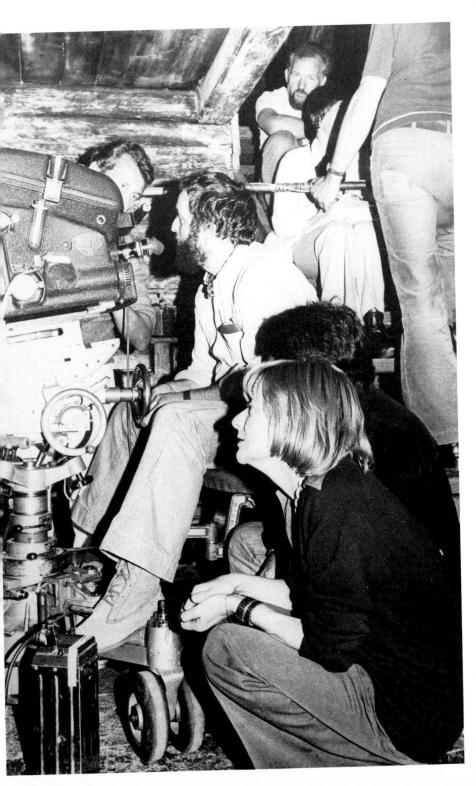

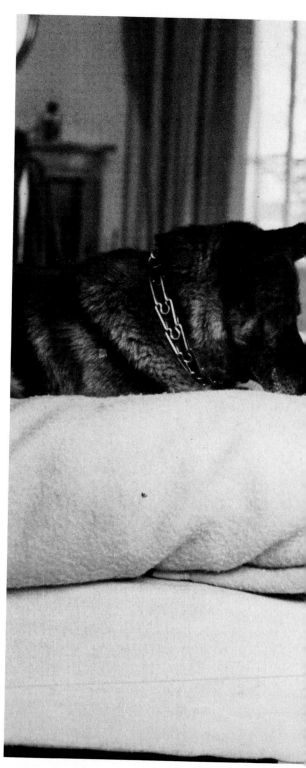

Reading Werther his favorite magazine.

With Hasty Flag and friends

*At the funeral of
Jean-Paul Sartre
April 19, 1980*

even people I don't know very well. They come to me, sit down and tell me their troubles. A psychiatrist friend once told me, "It's just as well you're not in practice; I'd lose all my patients." I'm also always delighted to meet people who are lively and cheerful. I love people who make me laugh. That's why I like Bernard Frank, for instance. He's well-balanced, good-hearted, reliable and he's funny. He also knows that you can lose friends by trying to understand them as well as by not trying. The people I love, the people I call my friends are sensitive and generous. Anyone who is capable of doing something for the sake of it, without looking for some moral or financial profit, immediately becomes my blood brother or sister.

I have lots of blood brothers and sisters all over the world. That's why I like to talk about nightbirds and party-goers, liars and drinkers. They're the only people with any imagination. You have to be a bit like that to get by in life, unless you want to be a hidebound conservative.

You seem to think that there are no "bad" people. Are there any bad characters in your novels?

My books do not have good and bad characters. They're all good. I believe that all human beings are weak and fragile. There always comes a point when the nightbirds want to break down and talk. They start by talking to you from their table and then they come and sit at yours. There's no need to ask questions. They want to explain things, tell their life stories or simply to be happy. The night is full of strangers who talk to me, often without even knowing who I am. It can be delightful or it can be painful, but it's never boring.

You make men sound like children.

Men are like children. They're so vulnerable. They want to play cowboys and they're afraid that no one will play with them. I feel sorry for men. They have more problems than women, because they now have to compete with women. What I mean is that in our day women have the right to do virtually everything men can do. But they can still be women, whereas men have to do the work they've always done and still have to prove their virility. Women decided to be strong just when men were beginning to feel weak. I think that our society treats men as badly as it treats women. But in my opinion, men suffer more. They're trapped by their work, by their political impotence and by their inability to change things. Women could help them. But they don't; they set themselves up as judges. It's all a bit ridiculous. Some women are so contradictory. They want both a good husband and a wonderful lover and all that implies. Materially, they want a peaceful life; emotionally, they want excitement. Women's attitudes have changed and they're going through a difficult phase. But it will all work out in the end.

What would your ideal man be like?

There is no such thing as an ideal man. The ideal man is the man you love at the moment. He might be childish. He might be eighty. There are no rules. He might be a young boy. He might be a grandfather. He might be protective or he might need protecting. Once you start talking about the ideal man, you get lost in generalities. I don't know any ideal men; I just know men. You go through several stages with men. You start out very young and you're a little frightened. Later on, when you're seventeen or eighteen you play with them and lead them on. Then you have real experiences. You begin to love one man and start acting aggressively or defensively. It depends how badly you burned your fingers in the past. Your ideas about men change as you go through life.

But surely there must be some constants.

Of course. Quite apart from the sexual side of things, women of all ages prefer certain men, men who enjoy being with women. They're quite rare. Lots of men love only their friends, their work or themselves. Only a few like being with women.

What about young men? They don't come off too well in your novels. They often seem to be drifting.

Young men are sad. Everyone makes mistakes when they're young. You always get your fingers burned. It's better to get that over with when you're young.

Doesn't physical beauty count at all?

Some women say that they don't care about good looks, that personality is what counts. But go to the beach and look at a man with personality, a paunch and thinning hair, and you'll soon find your eyes straying to the handsome lifeguard with the suntan. Physical beauty can be a matter of taste. If a woman is very beautiful, her beauty dominates her whole life. It's not everything – far from it – but it does influence her whole life.

Do you think that most men prefer any particular type of woman?

I'm convinced that most men like the Marilyn Monroe type. If they deny it, they're talking nonsense. Even so, I may be wrong. Men are looking for an image that corresponds to the image they have of themselves. It can get quite complicated: a weak man imagines himself to be strong, so he looks for a weak woman to protect. Then there'd be two weak people – who may be very happy together – or two failures. We all pay for our fantasies. The strong pay dearly too.

There are certain fantasies for which I have not yet paid, thank heaven, and others for which I have paid, in many ways that I believe to be too costly. But the word "fantasy" is totally subjective. For instance, to live for forty-five years with a man whom one no longer loves and to raise one's children and grand-children (some of whom one finds extremely unpleasant) seems to me the most preposterous of fantasies.

From a financial point of view I can't complain, I lead a very comfortable life. But I'm like everyone else in France; I don't like it when they take my money away from me and use it to build little missiles and atom bombs. I don't mind paying taxes if the money goes to those who need it: the old and the sick. But we live in a world where money is the only thing that counts.

What about publishers? Then we can talk about men and money at the same time.

When I left Julliard, all people could talk about were contracts. I prefer talking about my books. René Julliard had gone and so had Gisèle d'Assailly. None of the people I knew were there anymore. Then I met Henri Flammarion. He said, "My father used to have a dancer. At the time she was the only woman we published. That was Colette and we haven't had a dancer since she died." So I said, "You're in luck. I'm a very good dancer." He told me all the things I longed to hear; he wanted me to stay with Flammarion for the rest of my life. He would look after me when I was old and poor. Money wasn't that important. Relations between author and publisher should be based on complete trust. He gave me a feeling of moral security. I like feeling relaxed with people and not having to talk about money. I hate feeling I've been bought like a bag of coal.

In fact, you're fairly straightforward . . .

You must be joking. No one is straightforward. Some people seem to think I'm mad. Why do people always have to be so harsh? I may well be difficult, but I'm far from mad in the sense they mean.

I sometimes feel that you do in fact respect the conventions.

I respect the conventions in so far as they make my life easier. For instance, if I go to a nightclub, I don't drink myself under the table, simply because I'd have to pick myself up later. But I hate people who, for no apparent reason, unless it's their own stupidity, set themselves up as paragons of virtue.

The truth of the matter is that we all have the same problems and the same fear of living and dying.

They're even mean with the dead these days. I wrote about that in *The Heartkeeper*: "They're scarcely dead when they put them in tightly closed boxes and then put them in the ground. They put make-up on them, they display them under electric lights, they transform them and let them stiffen. I think we should expose them to the sun for ten minutes or take them to the sea, if that's what they liked. We should give them the earth for one last moment before they become part of it. Instead, they punish them for being dead. At best, they play Bach or some other religious music. It's usually the sort they didn't like."

POLITICS

People and political events interest me greatly. There are things I would die for. I'd be willing to risk my life for the people I love or to fight organized injustice.

That sounds like the beginning of an ideal. Do you think you have ideals?

Ideals depend on circumstances. You rebel against something and it becomes an ideal.

What do you see as the greatest injustice?

Social inequality.

Is that the real problem?

The real problems are very simple, and everyone knows what they are: death, illness, poverty, tiredness, boredom, sadness, loneliness . . .

Is everyone the same?

Everyone is different. Everyone wants different things. If only half the people who can feel and understand things would look around them, then perhaps things might begin to change.

Do you have a grudge against society?

Society steals people's time, the one thing that everyone owns and should be able to use as they wish. It's as if everyone had to sacrifice ten or fifteen years of their lives on the altar of the economy.

105

Not to mention retirement, which is usually very squalid. There's something wrong somewhere.

Just look at the television. It's dreadful. It gives people the illusion that they're communicating with each other, that they're sharing some kind of family life just because the four of them are sitting watching the same thing on television. It's ridiculous. Ask any four Catholics what they were thinking about during mass. They were all thinking about totally different things and not one of them was thinking about mass. It's terrible, the way four people can feel close to one another merely because they're sitting around the same television set. It means they don't have to talk to each other at all. When people sit around a table without a television set, they make an effort to talk to each other. They talk about the woman next door, the garden, the weather, all sorts of things. Television destroys communication and it's usually frighteningly mediocre. Either they're short of money or they're short of imagination. It's either those pathetic *It's a Knockout* things or intellectual complacency. People are so tired, so lonely. I once heard something quite insane on the radio. I don't often listen to it, but this was a "lonely hearts" program. There was nothing at all attractive about the man on offer. He'd lost his wife a year ago. He'd never loved anyone else and he wept for her every night. He was sixty. He wasn't good-looking, but he was virile, or so he said. He had seven children and a house with a little garden in Brussels. He wouldn't have a housekeeper; that was against his principles. He was describing a sort of hell on earth. And yet several women phoned in to talk to him. He asked one of them, "Do you smoke? If you do, the answer's no." Those women would have accepted anything rather than being alone.

Do you draw any political conclusions from your feelings of rebellion?

I always remember Marcelle Auclair saying, "Françoise Sagan is not a communist. She's an anarchist, a nihilist. In her own way, she hurls paper bombs which help to speed up the collapse of our society." That was in 1956. She didn't realize that the cracks were already there, that the world is going to collapse. People try to forget the H-bomb, but it's there. So are people's lives. For the moment.

And young people?

What have young people got to live for? Usually, they can't even find the jobs they want. The only ones with any hope left are the communists.

So your politics are instinctive rather than a matter of conviction.

I don't have much sense of history, so my political opinions are reactions to the things I hate: violence, poverty and hypocrisy.

How far would you go to defend your convictions?

I'm not a member of any political party, but I am committed to the Left. I hate killing and if there were a war, I'd leave the country. I don't know where I would go.

107

But if there was a fascist invasion, I'd stay and fight. I would fight against that.

With conviction or without any illusions?

You have to have convictions, but you musn't be taken in too easily. You know what Dostoevsky said: "It takes so long for our conviction to become a real part of us." The world is ruled by economic interests that ordinary mortals cannot understand. There again, everyone has something to worry about, his own little garden to cultivate. Intellectuals worry about "serious" things, shopkeepers worry about taxes and workers worry about not having a garden to worry about or not having a house to go with the garden they don't have.

Some years ago, you voted for de Gaulle.

I voted for him in 1965, because I thought he was the only one with real left-wing policies, even if they sometimes looked like a caricature of the real thing. If Mendès-France had been standing I'd have voted for him without any hesitation. What de Gaulle had done was in line with my own ideas: decolonization, contacts with the eastern bloc. I've often been opposed to de Gaulle, as when I signed the *Manifeste des 121*[6] in 1960. But in 1965 I had more faith in his policies than in Mitterand's.

Yet you voted for Mitterand in 1974.

Times had changed and he represented the modern

Left. But in 1965, the whole world was depressed and apathetic. De Gaulle was the only man who was prepared to take a stand to preserve the ideas of the Left, even though the way he did it may have looked strange to some people. I had no time for all the talk of his "destiny". But de Gaulle was a great actor, and he was the first to know it. He pulled it off; everyone was taken in. "Destiny" is Malraux's phrase. I don't like people with destinies. That's why I admire Sartre so much. He didn't have a destiny. He wasn't concerned with his public image, the way he looked or the direction his life might take. He wasn't concerned with the mark he would leave on history. His life was full of unexpected twists and turns. A rich disorganized life that wasn't planned in advance. I'm a great admirer of Sartre.

Sartre talks a lot about the writer's responsibility, about the need for the writer to commit himself.

The writer's responsibility . . . responsibility for what? I could never become a full-time activist like Jane Fonda or Joan Baez, but that doesn't mean that I don't live in a perpetual state of indignation. Their problem is different. They live in a country with a serious race problem and until very recently the war in Vietnam was an everyday fact of life. I saw the police raids during the Algerian war. I saw the police charge on the Boulevard Bonne-Nouvelle and unarmed Algerians being machine-gunned and I decided we had to put an end to it. So I became involved in the anti-war movement. I was involved in the campaign over Djamila Boupacha[7]. My flat was even bombed by the O.A.S.[8]

But do you agree with Sartre that the writer must be involved in politics?

Whether a writer does or does not become involved in politics is up to him. The writer is free. If he feels concerned about political events, then he becomes involved. It's only logical. But if he feels that his sole concern is aesthetic problems, he doesn't and that's all there is to it. A writer is a wild animal locked up alone in a cage. Whether or not he looks outside depends upon what's happening.

Then you don't feel any desire to change society?

It seems to me that the society we live in is a complete and utter mess. It causes people a lot of pain. Personally, I feel somewhat distanced from it all. I sometimes feel a little out of date. The way of life I prefer is not today's way of life. The same few men always have the power. The same few men always do the bombing, whether it's in Vietnam or anywhere else. It's scandalous, horrible and inevitable. But it's no worse than the Inquisition or the wars of religion.

The present is no worse than the past. What about the future?

Either people will be reduced to total degradation, something disastrous will happen or there'll be a nuclear war. Or even something else . . . I don't know. You're lucky if you can believe that man has any future at all, let alone a happy future.

I am pessimistic about civilization or about what it

means in practical terms. People do not have time to get to know each other, to understand each other. They simply do not have the time. I'm convinced that very few people make love at night. They're all too tired.

May '68 was fantastic. We've never known such freedom. The tragedy of it was that it was the poor people, the workers who suffered as a result, not the students. But there was such a fantastic feeling of freedom.

Was May '68 revolt the answer?

May '68 was the only answer to the political confusion. But it had serious consequences for the poor. It's not so important for people who pay more and more in tax; they can afford it. A series of explosions is no answer. What we need is one big radical explosion.

Are you doing anything toward it?

I'm not sure that I have any influence on society. To go back to Sartre for a moment, his ability to work and his intelligence mean that he can write novels and be involved in politics. I can't do both. There are things I hate, papers I will not read and people I cannot stand. But that's just a negative attitude. Many people say that's not enough. I don't know who's right. Morally, it doesn't bother me any more than not being able to fly. And I *would* like to be able to fly. Socially, it does bother me, because you can't avoid being aware of some of the terrible things that happen. But I don't think I would hesitate if the situation became worse and forced me to take sides.

It's the same with the Women's Liberation Movement. Given my privileged position, the problems the Women's Movement is raising don't concern me directly. They're obviously right to say that women do more work than men; they come home from work and then have to start dealing with the children, doing the housework and all the rest of it. Being a beast of burden is no life.

What about abortion?

Abortion is a question of class. If you're rich, there's no problem. You go to Switzerland or somewhere and you come back in one piece. If you're poor, have five kids and a careless husband, you go to see the woman in the corner shop. She knows a nurse who knows someone else . . . and you get butchered.

You have no right to have a child unless you really want it. I think it's shameful to bring a human being into the world unless you really intend to make it happy. Obviously, you can't be certain that you will, but you can decide to try at all costs. Some women are trapped once they become pregnant.

Didn't you sign the abortion manifesto[9]?

Yes I signed it. It was necessary and it served its purpose. Then there's all this talk of women liberating themselves from men. Some men have always been stronger than women and have always treated them badly. And there have always been women who could lead men by the nose and treat them like dirt. The

Women's Liberation Movement often seems to miss the point. People lead impossibly hard lives. The Women's Liberation Movement says that they come home and watch television instead of making love because they have sexual problems. It's not true; they're simply worn out.

Do you take the Movement's other aims more seriously?

Some of its aims are perfectly valid: equal pay, child allowances. It's true that the law works in favor of men, but it has been changed. Perhaps it can be changed again, perhaps not. I suppose my views are out of date and typically French, but I really do not believe that women will get anywhere by uniting against men. If they do, it will only be in legal terms. And the law isn't everything.

So what's to be done with men?

We have to talk to men and make them understand. I think that the idea of a war between the sexes is out of date. Just look at couples of twenty or twenty-five; one does the washing up and the other puts the dishes away. At that level at least there are fewer problems than there used to be.

The system has to be changed. The economic problems have to be resolved.

It sounds as if the only thing that matters to you is freedom. Your freedom or that of other people?

I want people to respect my freedom, so I always respect theirs. It's a question of finding a balance between the two, of not desperately wanting the things you don't have and regretting the things you do have, of being realistic and taking things as they come.

A lot of people would either laugh or get very angry to hear me – of all people – talking about balance. They think that leading a balanced life means doing sensible things and being terribly unbalanced, doing stupid things and getting away with them. When I talk about balance I mean going to bed at night without feeling frightened and waking up in the morning without feeling depressed. A feeling of harmony between your life and the way you see yourself. "Balance" means avoiding situations which might become intolerable.

Do you ever feel something of an outsider?

Being a writer means lots of things. It means that you have to be alone. It also means that you need constant change, and that, from time to time, you have blind spots. But I don't think I occupy any special place. I know my place in the sense that I take up so many square meters and that I was born in such and such a year. I know my place in terms of time and space, but not in social terms. I relate quite well to myself, because I don't find myself unbearable. On the other hand, I'm cold toward myself because I don't find myself all that interesting. I talk to myself: "Oh, I've an appointment now. You don't look too well, you know. You really ought to think about it, you know."

External events are always accidents. The real drama is everyday life . . . getting up, going to bed. In between you fuss around and let things slide. Sometimes you realize that, but not very often. You realize it when you're alone in bed at night and feeling sad.

LIKES AND DISLIKES

What would it be like to be happy?

Being really happy means waking up in a good mood. I take everything seriously, especially people and literature. But I never take myself seriously.

Have you changed over the last twenty years?

When I was twenty I could change because of another person. I could discover things through other people. I don't think I could do that now. My life may change. I might be happy or I might be unhappy, but I can't change the reflexes; that's the real me. The only person who can change me now is me.

But you still have fears and joys.

Fears? . . . I sometimes wake up at eight o'clock in the morning, wondering why I exist and why I'll die. Joys? . . . Having a drink with someone, talking to them, hugging them. My joys and fears take so many forms that they become interchangeable: yesterday's fear becomes today's joy.

I get exasperated with pretentiousness, inadequacy and with all the pseudo-intellectualism, the pseudo-language that seems to be flourishing today. Things like that drive me up the wall.

Do you become attached to things or places?

I hate *things*. I don't like having things of my own. I don't have time to own things. I enjoy reading books but I give them away once I've read them. I do keep some old things with me, my old piano, a couch that sags, I'm always moving house; a different window, a different view. I don't actually have anything to do with the practical side of it. When the moving men arrive, I disappear. I come back and someone says "This is your room" and I go to bed. I love that. I'm like a gypsy. I'd love to live in hotels, but you can't if you have a child.

And what about fashion?

I don't like fashion. I avoid it. I once suggested to the editor of a women's magazine that I write a special anti-issue: how to become lazy, old, fat, ugly and miserable in a fortnight. I don't think she saw the joke. I'm terrified of women who follow fashion, dress like everyone else and let themselves be brain-washed by the "advice" they get from women's magazines. Girls should be taught not to believe in silly things like being beautiful, relaxed and happy.

Your dislikes are stronger than your likes.

Lets say that I talk less about the things I love. I hate sweet smells, plastic and television. I simply cannot stand television. I hate meanness, envy and intolerance. I cannot stand people who willfully behave as if they were badly brought up and humiliate people in front of me. I loathe racism in all its forms. I hate conformism, people who have no imagination and people who think they have the right to judge others. And I dislike arrogant, fatuous people and that stupid fear that makes everyone want to feel superior to everyone else simply because they're Aryan, Jewish, rich or poor. Some people will use anything to make themselves look smarter than the next man. And finally, I loathe complacent ignorance.

I only go to dinner with people I know well. I know that they have their doubts and question things too. I'm very restless. People who make up their minds about something once and for all are not my type. Things that are cold and neutral bore me to tears. The strange thing is that people who are kind and affec-. tionate, people who do understand others – and I think most people are like that – are usually afraid to show what they are feeling. It's as if they thought it would devalue them in the eyes of others or even in their own eyes. All the kind, vulnerable people, all the losers will win in the end. You become invulnerable when you lay down your arms. I discovered that a long time ago.

Do you ever get angry?

I do, but not more than once or twice a year. When I get angry I lose control of myself and I don't like that. But I simply cannot bear to talk about certain topics. I refuse to listen to people with racist or right-wing ideas. Certain types of arguments – sophistry for one – get on my nerves. I become so afraid of what I might say that I hurry people away and then I hurt myself. I put my hand through the window and cut it. Then I can breathe again. If I didn't do that I'd suffocate. But first, I politely show everyone out. My anger just sweeps over me. The same sort of anger brought about my grandfather's death: he got angry because a taxi-driver took the wrong turn.

I may look calm, but when I'm sad, the only way I will get back to normal is to overdo things. I have to feel exhausted before I can relax. I have to be worried before I can calm down. I always start my novels when I'm completely depressed.

The thought of ending up with set ideas terrifies me. The thought of not being able to change, to understand things, the thought of becoming set in my ways like so many other people, and not being able to laugh. Calamities always make me laugh. I can't help but laugh when I think that I once told Von Karajan that my favorite piece of Bruckner was "The Trout Quintet"!

How do you see yourself?

I see myself as being carefree rather than trivial, but I'd rather be thought of as trivial than as a hard-headed intellectual.

I get very bored listening to all these liberated women rabbiting on, all so sure of themselves, so responsible and spending eight hours a day cooped up in a little office. I like to dream, to do nothing. I like to watch the time go by without feeling bored or empty. That's real liberation. I'm incapable of forcing myself to do things I don't want to do. I take life as it comes, I look left and right, but I don't look ahead and I don't look back over my shoulder.

Are you as lazy as people say you are?

It's very difficult to be very lazy. It takes a lot of imagination to do nothing and you have to be sufficiently self-confident not to have a bad conscience. You have to have a taste for life, so that every minute is complete in itself and so you don't have to keep saying "I've done this or that." You need strong nerves to do nothing. Being lazy also means that other people's opinions don't matter. Nor does the idea of always having to prove yourself.

I may be lazy, but I enjoy working, too.The pleasure I derive from my work overcomes the laziness and I work for a while. But the best thing about me is that I'm a reasonably pleasant person.

You say you're not very adult. Haven't you aged at all?

When you're young, you have an appetite for life. As you grow older you become harder to please and you begin to realize that you are born and that you die. In the meantime you live. As you grow older you have fewer pleasures and more interests. I'm not afraid of growing old. What does frighten me is that going out will cease being an adventure, even if the adventure is only someone smiling back at me. I think the fear of old age is closely connected with physical desire. It's terrifying to think that you'll no longer be sexually attractive. It would be rather sad to die at fifty or to live for something else. No more strangers! The best place to talk to someone is in bed. It would really hurt if the adventure went out of my life. But you can always act your age in one way or another. When I'm fifty, my son will be twenty-five and, who knows? I may have children clambering all over me.

Would you like to be a grandmother?

I don't know. I might be delighted, I might be horrified. No, I don't know. And then, when life loses some of its immediate charms, I'll write a good book.

In that case you'll have a happy old age. What would be your vision of an unhappy old age?

The worst thing I can imagine is ending up in the gallery of prize-winners along with Marguerite Duras, Françoise Mallet-Joris and Geneviève Dormann . . . all four of us resigned to our fate. That's my vision of Apocalypse, like something out of Bosch. A vision of horror for all four of us.

You're not interested in honors then?

I've known about honors for twenty years and for twenty years they've left me cold. I don't think I'll change my views now. Honors mean different things to different people. For some people, ten pages in *Life* is a great honor. Others dream of the *Légion d'Honneur* or a knighthood. I might settle for the Order of Agricultural Merit, just for a joke. Or the Ministry of Practical Jokes. But none of that has any importance. Why were we born? What are we doing here? Where are we going? One day there will be no more Françoise Sagan.

What is your favorite pastime?

My favorite pastime is watching time go by, taking my time, wasting my time, moving against the rhythm of time. I hate things that leave me no time to myself. That's why I like the night. The day is one long, dreary round of appointments. At night, time becomes a calm sea. It goes on for ever. I like to see the sun come up before I go to bed.

The question of time is always nagging at me. People don't have time to sit and let time go by. Each and every minute should be a gift, but it's just a breathing space between two other minutes. Every single minute ought to be full of happiness, silence or some real feeling. It doesn't matter, so long as it is full. People no longer have time to have real feelings.

I have time. But I realize to what extent that's a privilege, and a passion. In any case, if something cannot become a passion, it ceases to be a privilege.

I think the best way to waste time is to try to save time. It's rather like that stupid thing you see at fairgrounds. You have to walk forward along a belt moving in the opposite direction. You run to try to catch up with yourself, stumble, catch hold of the rail and fall. The one thing I regret is that I will never have time to read all the books I would like to read. Watching the clouds go by or doing stupid things – not that I think they are stupid – is not a waste of time, because that way I can *watch* it going by. The important thing is to think of time as a gift and not as an arrow.

These days, solitude is a luxury too. People are rarely alone; they're either at the office or at home with the family. I've heard friends, both married men and women, say "Traffic jams? You don't know what you're talking about. They're very peaceful. It's the only time you're alone." No one can contact them, so they're alone and free for an hour, bumper to bumper.

Some women complain about being lonely . . . but that's because they don't think about it. I've learned to be alone and I've learned to love it. Being alone is a kind of self-consciousness, an awareness of something permanent, something that you can't talk about. It's almost biological. I often feel loneliest when I'm with a group of friends. I like that kind of loneliness. Sometimes a nightclub can be the loneliest place in the world. I sometimes feel an urge to live alone, to be quite independent and autonomous, to have time to myself, to get a grip on myself and to meet strangers. I feel like seeing things, going for walks or travelling. I could spend a week in a boring little town in Belgium, go to India, Russia or Tibet, just to tear myself away from things that have become too familiar.

Sometimes I really do need to be alone, but I never forget Stendhal's words, "Solitude can give you everything but character."

I make a distinction between spending an afternoon alone listening to records and drinking tea and being really alone. Everyone knows what it is like to be alone: there's no escape from it and it's no luxury. We are born alone and we die alone. I'm convinced that everyone "feels" lonely and is deeply unhappy about it.

We try to think about it as little as possible. We try to fill the void. Usually with love, which always gets in the way. I think many things are desirable: love, admiration, respect. But love is the most important of them all.

LOVE

What people usually call love is a selfish feeling, a desire to own someone. But it can also mean being kind and gentle to someone and missing them when they're not there. The love you feel for someone may turn into a feeling of friendship. Or there again, friendship may develop into love.

Love is not at all peaceful. Love is usually a battle. A battle in which each partner tries to enslave the other. Even the most generous attitudes are based upon jealousy, possessiveness and trying to own someone. Like all battles, it claims its victims. One partner is always more in love than the other. Someone gets hurt, or is hurt because he or she is hurting someone else. Fortunately, it's not always the same person and the roles do get reversed. But kindness leads to an acceptance of the other person, to trust. The trouble is that people are always looking for something they can't find. Very few people are satisfied with their position or their material life. They try to make up for that in their love affairs, because they want to be winners in at least one area. But there's nothing to win. You win by giving yourself, by letting yourself go. Then there's the "knack" of love affairs; giving your partner a semblance of freedom so that he begins to wonder if you do actually love him. I don't care much for that. It's only natural to assume that if someone lives with you, sleeps with you and, above all, laughs with you that he does love you. So why should you imagine that he's going to run off with someone else. It's only logical.

Relating to someone as a human being means being on terms of equality, being able to trust them and talk to them regardless of love. Call it friendship. Love without friendship is a terrible thing. If you fall in love with an image that someone is projecting, everything becomes distorted. Loving someone means loving their happiness. Loving someone who loves you involves rights and duties. But the duties come first. You have to make sure that the person you love is as happy as you are.

My ideas about love have not changed greatly over the years. I've always believed that it is a very important part of people's lives. Perhaps I've learned to respect other people and perhaps I've gained some idea, some knowledge of how completely vulnerable people are. I'd never realized that people could be so hurt. I never knew that people could hurt you so much, that you could feel such unhappiness, such panic or such despair.

It took me a very long time to understand this, but I've finally come to realize there is a form of absolute. That word used to terrify me, but now I see it as a good way to live. What I didn't know about was kindness, that mixture of warmth and resignation, that acceptance of the other person. It's not a quality, it's an instinct. People who are not kind are asking you for something that you cannot give them. Kindness is usually connected with inner strength. In terms of love it means affection, understanding, all the things that are meant by cherishing someone.

What importance do you give to sexuality?

It means everything and nothing. It's indispensable, but it can never be enough. Roger Vailland used to say, "Love is what happens between two people who love one another." There is too much talk of sexuality today. It's such a heavy word, it always sounds so clinical, so pharmaceutical. Sexuality and love are not always the same thing.

I can't remember who it was that said, "I often make love, but I never talk about it", but it's a good saying. Sexuality and eroticism are not things to be displayed in public. They are secret, lyrical ceremonies of the night, black, red, gold and black, like a mass. Some feelings should be kept secret; defeat, the totally naked face of pleasure when you at last lose control and give in to it. Yes, a mass. In the past, I always liked mass. It was very beautiful, but it would have been very embarrassing if it had been filmed.

You mean you don't like being forced into being a voyeur?

No. That's the one area in theatre and cinema where convention and the absence of truth embarrass me most.

Because you can simulate tears, pain, love, but not pleasure.

Real physical pleasure cannot be simulated. Whenever I see someone trying to do so I feel as if I were watching someone commit an indiscretion or even sacrilege.

I saw a private showing of *Sunday, Bloody Sunday*. I find most erotic films boring and cliché-ridden, but I found that story of a young man torn between a man and a woman more daring and more disturbing, in an intelligent way, then all those films of people rolling around on fur rugs. It's a very difficult subject and I

129

was very impressed by the way the director and the actors never seemed to be embarrassed. They didn't seem to look down on it.

You weren't embarrassed by the scene where the young man kisses him on the mouth?

No, I wasn't embarrassed. He's bisexual, but he never lies to himself or to anyone else about it. He has no feeling of shame.

You say you're in favor of being frank and against exhibitionism. But you're a writer and many people say that writing is the worst form of exhibitionism.

No, it isn't. There's a world of difference between writing and those films where you can practically count the blackheads on the wretched man's back as he pants away on top of some woman. Writing is a way of looking at things and translating them. That doesn't mean you always talk about yourself. Writing is a tool you use, like a magnifying glass or a telescope. But when I'm in a *salon* and the people sitting opposite me start flirting and kissing, I feel embarrassed. I feel like telling them to go home. Either I shouldn't be there or they shouldn't be there.

I feel the same way in the cinema. But in the cinema you can't get away from seeing eroticism, blood and violence.

This flood of eroticism has changed people's attitudes, not their nature. They feel that they have to be sexy in the same way that they have to be slim and suntanned, or even happy. It's funny and at the same time it's horrible. When the dinner party is over, people start pairing off and going home together. You can tell that he's going to play at being a man and she's going to play at being a woman, at writhing and moaning. They're going to play at sex object and dominant male and God knows what else. I often wonder which of them is going to play at being a human being. I have grave doubts about it all. This odd mixture of exhibitionism and vulgarized Freudian theories makes people think that they have to make love, that they have to let others know that they're having an affair, even if they don't enjoy it. I'm sure they're lying to themselves. It's as if a woman without a lover must be frustrated or as if a man without a mistress can't be a real man.

The act of love is an act of pleasure. You either want someone or you don't. Sexuality is a taste, not an obligation. If you love someone and he's there with you, that's fine. If there's no one there, you go to sleep and that's fine too. Anyone can spend a peaceful three months alone. Looking for pleasure is the best way to ensure you won't find it. There can be no pleasure unless two people are physically – and often intellectually – attracted to one another, unless they feel happy and warm together, and enjoy talking far into the night.

I loathe this flood of eroticism. It annoys me. Suggestion is more important than provocation. It's so boring, so unimaginative. If you really want eroticism, you should go back to de Sade and Sacher-Masoch, tie people up in corners, beat them and then rub salt in the wounds. All these displays of naked people making love are so boring. What has it got to do with me if they make love with the light on or off, if she wears a night-gown or not, if they wear pajama tops or not, if they talk, cry out or whatever?

The way sexuality is displayed all over the place destroys the secrecy, the beauty of love. In the past, you might see two people glance at each other. You didn't know they were lovers, but something about the way they looked at each other made you think, "Oh, they're in love, they want each other." There was something magnificent about that. But nowadays people rush into each other's arms and start kissing, as if they always had to be proving something, as if they always had to be proving themselves.

You sound as if you'd like to go back to the age of romanticism.

Nowadays, romanticism is something to be kept in check, something to be punished. That's a shame, because we all have passions and passions lead to romanticism. Romanticism is what happens when the heart follows the imagination.

I haven't had a great many passionate affairs in my life . . . one or two, perhaps three. They are fantastic, but you shouldn't have them too often.

I might well fall madly in love with some idiot who'll whisk me off to Brazil the day after tomorrow. It's always possible, touch wood. Given the way I live, he wouldn't have much chance of whisking me off to Brazil, but sometimes you do get swept off your feet like that. But some things will take you a lot farther than Brazil. Fall in love with an alcoholic and you'll go farther than Brazil, I can tell you. You can go ten times around the world without ever leaving your room.

None of my affairs have ever lasted more than seven years. They say your body renews itself every seven years. The beginning is always marvelous. The middle of the affair is even better. The end depends on who tires first. But whatever happens, the end of the affair is always sad. I always go on loving . . . even after the affair is over. Afterward the head and the heart are no longer properly synchronized. You go on living intellectually, but not emotionally. But something remains, like a scar. There's nothing sad about that. A ritual scar is the most beautiful of decorations.

Do you have any scars?

Five or six, I should think.

Do you think fidelity is essential? And what do you think about jealousy?

Fidelity is possible, even if it is difficult. Jealousy is horrible. I have seen people who were jealous and I've always thought it was horribly destructive. They get hurt, they hurt other people and everything is warped. It becomes very frightening when someone accepts jealousy and begins to see it as a virtue to be defended.

The terrible thing about people is their possessiveness, in love and in life as a whole. They want to keep everything to themselves, money, jobs, everything. They forget to allow other people their freedom. They forget about other people's happiness. All they think about is themselves, about owning things and putting them away tidily. Pocket money in this drawer, handkerchiefs in this one and pleasure in this one. Everything has to be pigeon-holed once and for all. Their one real passion is security and they satisfy it by owning things.

Love means trusting people. A love affair based upon jealousy is doomed from the start. Jealousy means struggles and fights. Realizing that you're important to someone because he's jealous may well be exhilarating. It certainly is a sign of love, but it's a sign that it's already dying. All the little games people play when they're jealous are so pathetic. Lovers have to trust one another completely. If someone cheats on you, that's too bad. In any case, the people who do the cheating suffer more than the people they cheat on. Lots of people want a love affair to be a paroxysm of feeling and use jealousy to get what they want. Their partners are fascinated, but only by the violence. Oh yes, it's a human relationship, but so is the relationship between master and slave and the relationship between torturer and victim.

It's true that a woman feels very unhappy if she doesn't sense that the man she loves wants to have her and to keep her. Jealousy ought to be something gay. The man ought to make light-hearted scenes. That way you would feel that it is something serious, that he did notice you looking at so and so. But he doesn't have to make a dreadful scene every time it happens.

I think a jealous man should hide his jealousy. If he can't he should leave. Going away is a healthy thing for a jealous man to do. It makes him feel better because being near his mistress feeds his jealousy. If the one you love is near you, you automatically search the town for him. If he's miles away and you can't do anything about it, your imagination begins to dry up. And for once, that's healthy.

I don't have a jealous nature, but I have felt jealous when I've been forced to see things with my own eyes. If I'd been left to my own devices, I'd never have seen a thing. One day I met the man I loved with a woman he'd told me was a friend from the country. I believed him. Like all good liars, I'm very credulous. My friends were horrified.

I was hurt, but to tell the truth, I was disappointed rather than jealous. I thought, "What a stupid thing to do. Why did he do it? Why didn't he tell me? Why?"

Jealousy is not a feeling I enjoy. I always try to hide the fact that I'm physically jealous from myself. I try to turn it into disappointment or sadness. Even so, yes, I *do* know what it's like to be physically jealous.

You can always hide things. It's the least you can do. When that sort of thing happens, I begin to despise the man. It doesn't revive my love; it kills it.

If a man cheats on you he can tell people about it or laugh at you behind your back. That really is a betrayal. If he takes her to meet your friends, it's an insult and that is quite unforgivable. But what can you do if he spends an hour with another woman? You might not even know, but even if you do find out, what can you do about it? That's not very serious. But it is hard to take when the man you love begins to get interested in another woman. There have been times when I've not slept for two nights because I was jealous. There have been other times when I've not slept for a week because I was so happy.

When you're happy, you don't need food or sleep. You can stay awake all night, like the birds. It does happen. It's a state of grace and it has incalculable results. The happiness of people who are in love and who are loved shows in their faces. They have an expression that's at once very far away and very much part of the present.

Happiness means that you never have to feel ashamed of what you're doing. You're not ashamed and you're not proud; you simply feel at ease with yourself. It means enjoying yourself, talking to people you love. Happiness is the sea, the sun and the grass.

I feel much more at ease when I'm happy than when I'm unhappy. Some people enjoy being unhappy, but I loathe it. I think you become a better, more intelligent person when you are happy. Being unhappy makes you ill. You close in upon yourself.

I believe there are two kinds of happiness. Happiness can come as a complete surprise, like a bolt from the blue, like a love that is shared. Or it can be a way of loving life. If you treat life well, life is usually good to you. And I love life. There's a long-standing affair between us.

What about marriage?

I believe that marriage is a good thing. It must be wonderful to share your life with someone you love. But living with someone is a terrifying thought. Basically, the problem is very simple. Either you choose to live with someone and make concessions, or the boredom of living together outweighs the pleasure it gives you. It might even be possible to love someone for life.

Everything is possible. But there are no recipes for a long, happy love affair.

You've had several husbands of one kind or another. How do you get on with them now?

I'm still on friendly terms with my former husbands. And I still have the same men friends. I ought to build a sort of pen for them. The trouble is, it might become a little crowded.

At what point do you feel that an affair is over?

You should break it off the moment you begin to feel bored or chilly, the moment you begin to feel uncomfortable. If you don't, something begins to gnaw away at you. You hurt your partner because he doesn't know; he can't tell what's happening. Either that or you develop a taste for hurting or being hurt, and that's no better.

Is boredom a serious problem?

Boredom is a bug you pick up. If a woman tells me, "I'm bored at home. My husband bores me to death. My children are getting on my nerves," I say "Go out to work." If she says, "I'm perpetually bored", I say "Jump out of the window." You always think of people who are bored as going around with long faces and looking apathetic. But the people who are really bored are the ones who haven't discovered what to do with their lives. In terms of love, boredom means that you no longer enjoy being together.

There must be some deep, underlying reason why people come to the end of their emotional, intellectual and imaginative resources after six or seven years. Being even-tempered is all very well, until you begin to wish that something would happen. The cells of the body are renewed every seven years, so why shouldn't the cells of the heart be renewed too? A change of heart is hard on everybody. . . . It is hard on me, too. If it weren't for that, I would be altogether faithful.

The only solution is to turn your husband into a lover. You have to get a divorce first. (Or perhaps the real solution is not to get married in the first place.) I've been married twice – both civil marriages. The first time I believed in marriage. I believed I should live with the man I loved and I thought that it would last. The second time, I did it out of kindness, because he wanted to. I also felt responsible toward my son. I was expecting a baby. Bob was delighted at the idea of having a child and my mother would have been dreadfully upset at the idea of my being an unmarried mother.

Not exactly the ideal marriage.

Why not? I loved Bob more than anyone else. In an ideal world, it would be like that every morning and every night. You would always be living with the best man in the world. The attraction would have to be very strong for that to happen. Some nights you're tired and all you want to do is go to sleep. The only person you love is yourself. You know that you're going to sleep with someone out of habit and it doesn't matter if he's restless, talks in his sleep or sleeps like a log. That fam-

138

iliarity, that bodily affection, if you like, means that you can sleep with a husband you've known for five years and not with Gary Cooper or Kirk Douglas.

A good husband is a good lover who knows what he's doing. You could also say that he's a good lover to whom you're legally bound. I don't think there's any intrinsic difference between a lover and a husband. In the days when women didn't go out to work, they were married for life. But nowadays there's no difference between having a husband and having a regular lover.

If I were cynical, I would say that a woman should have both a good husband and a lover. But I'm not cynical so I'll just say that a woman should have a lover who's a good husband and a husband who's a good lover, perhaps both.

As a rule, women stay with husbands longer than with lovers. Presumably that's because, contrary to what one might think, a lover is more finicky and more jealous than a husband and is more bothered about observing the conventions. You fall for a kind, gentle man, only to find that he's a monster. A lover feels more vulnerable, more threatened than a husband. A lot of it has to do with the setting. A husband can always turn over and go to sleep. He's in his own home and he feels safe. He knows he'll always have a bed to sleep in. Men are as much creatures of habit as women. That's the disadvantage: a husband who feels he's married for life, who feels sure of you, tends to go to sleep too quickly. You should always keep a husband – or anyone else for that matter – guessing. Treat him kindly, but keep him guessing. But at the same time, you have to believe that you'll be with him until the day you die.

Men are creatures of habit, but they don't always like to be sure of everything. Personally, I'm too fond of happiness to have desires that cannot be realized. Freedom means being free to enjoy yourself and to be moved. Faulkner said something to the effect that the best way to live is to enjoy our allotted span, breathe, live and be aware of it. Perhaps the quest for happiness means constantly living with the idea of death. I don't find that an unpleasant idea. If it weren't for death, which puts an end to everything, people would become impossibly pretentious. It's a stimulating idea.

DEATH AND GOD

Death itself is the most frightening thing in the world. I sometimes wake up in the middle of the night and think, "One day, you won't be here any more". It's silly really; I don't know why I do it. No one can accept the idea that day by day they're getting nearer to death, not if they think about it at night. Or at any other time, come to that. But sometimes you can share the fear. You can lean on someone else for a while. But when you die, you are alone. Think of Rimbaud dying in hospital in Marseilles. He said to his sister, "I am dying and you walk out into the sunshine." He was furious.

Sometimes I lie on my bed and think, "I'm going to die. The people around me are going to die." That makes me want to do a thousand and one things. I often hear people talking to me and I suddenly realize that they're going to die too. So I begin to listen to them in a new way. I see them as they really are. I want to make them stop acting out roles, to ask them why they're making so much fuss, why they take themselves so seriously and put on all those airs. I want to tell them what's really important. I want them to have a drink. I love those fleeting moments when people have had a few drinks and begin to be a bit unsteady. They let themselves go, stop acting and take their clothes off. They take off their masks and begin to say something real. Sometimes they begin to talk metaphysics. That can be very stimulating.

God, of course, is one answer, but not my answer. Mauriac used to say that I was closer to grace than many practicing Christians. I liked Mauriac; he had an extraordinarily lively mind. I like the idea that, somewhere in my life, somewhere inside me, there is something that is still not satisfied, something that is still calling out for something.

I used to believe in God; I spent my girlhood in convents. Then I began to read Camus and Sartre. A visit to Lourdes completed the process. I stopped believing in God when I was thirteen or fourteen. It was very sudden. It always is at that age.

In some ways, believing in God today would make life easier. In other ways, it would make it more complicated. I've nothing against Christians; all people with a passion are worthy of respect. But now I am a complete atheist. I tend to agree with Faulkner, who once said that idleness produces our most attractive qualities: contemplation, good humor, laziness, leaving people alone, good mental and physical digestion.

As to the current supposition that "God is dead," I should like to point out that there are still a goodly number of persons who have not received the announcement.

HAPPINESS

It's curious. Legend has it that you're a town dweller who lives by night. But when you speak of happiness and time you begin to sound like someone who lives in the country, someone who lives very close to nature. Where are your roots?

I love the countryside. I was brought up there until I was fifteen and I often go back. I like the fresh air. I need fresh air and grass. I like riding and going for long walks without seeing a soul. I love the rivers and the smell of the earth. I belong to the land.

My great ambition has always been to have a house of my own in the country. A house with lots of rooms, a safe place, somewhere to drop anchor. I'm not afraid of dying, but I start to worry the moment I catch a cold. And unfortunately, the only houses I like are old and drafty.

The house at Equemauville in Normandy is the only thing I've succeeded in keeping. I lose things; they slip through my fingers. I bought the house on a sudden impulse and I've had it ever since. It's drafty and dilapidated, but it's isolated and beautiful. It dates from the nineteenth century. It's very long and has lots of rooms. It used to belong to Lucien Guitry, who mentions it in his books. Alphonse Allais has written about it too.

I relate very well to animals. I've always kept cats and dogs. It's terrible trying to sit in front of a log fire when there are dogs around – they always choose the best spot to sit. I remember going to a nightclub in Montparnasse with some friends once. There were some performing dogs. Youki was fast asleep with his head on my knee, but all at once he woke up, bounded up onto the stage and started chasing the other dogs. It was so funny! Youki was a dog I got from the Society for the Protection of Animals. He was a mongrel, but I was very fond of him. I lost him.

A long time ago, someone gave me a horse called Pinpin. He was lonely, so I bought a donkey to keep him company. Pinpin died and then the donkey was lonely. So I bought a horse which began to feel lonely when the donkey died. I bought another donkey. Now the pair of them are just like Laurel and Hardy.

Perhaps we could talk about music and paintings.

I'm very fond of music. I'm one of those people whose hearing is more developed than their visual senses. I need to have music in the background. The phonograph is a wonderful invention. It makes music so accessible – you can listen to it all day long. If you want to look at pictures you have to go to galleries, push through crowds of people and dodge the attendants when you want a cigarette. I'm too lazy to do that. In any case, there's a museum without walls inside my head. I create my own paintings when I write. How could I write music inside my head? I don't hear symphonies in my head when I go to bed at night. But if I simply close my eyes, I can see suns and moons.

I adore Mozart and I go through phases of enthusiasm for other composers: Bruckner, Mahler, opera. When I saw *La Traviata* in New York, something clicked inside me. I have a painting called "Night at the Opera". It always makes me laugh. It's not worth anything. None of the paintings I own are worth anything. I have another painting I like. It's a Dutch interior,

148

people sitting down to eat. But they all look so odd. They must be mad, or at least a little zany. I had a little brass plaque engraved, the sort they have in museums. It says, "Dinner at the Van Zanies". Would you believe that some people look at it very knowingly and then "Ah, I see you have a Van Zany".

There's one important person in your life whom you rarely mention – your son.

I know how a tree must feel when it puts out a new branch. That's how I felt when I had my child.

I used to dream of having a child. Dreams are like pictures. I would dream of being on a beach with a little boy beside me. Inside my head I could see it. A picture of me, a man and a child.

When he was born and they gave him to me to hold, I felt extraordinarily euphoric. It's a purely physiological reaction that doctors are familiar with but which men can never know. I think I felt euphoric because the delivery was over rather than because I had a baby in my arms, but I was very happy for an hour or so. Then I went to sleep. Afterward, I was very depressed for a fortnight. Doctors have an explanation for that too. It's not psychological; it's a question of physical fatigue. All women experience it.

Wanting to have children is a very old, primitive instinct. It has something to do with wanting to see a human being you've made.

Children are very important, but a woman is still a woman, even if she never has children. She's a woman as long as she loves someone. A selfish old woman with an old cat is still a woman and goes on having

149

imaginary children.

Maternal instincts are something you either have or have not. Do you agree?

If maternal instincts mean loving your child, yes. If they mean turning him into an object that belongs to you, no.

What sort of mother are you?

I worry when Denis is ill and I never stop thinking about him. I'm overjoyed when he's with me and I miss him when he's not there. But I don't smother him. Having a child has changed my life. I have to think about things I used to be able to ignore. I might be in a plane crash, so I take out insurance whenever I fly. For the first time in my life, I feel that there is someone who has the right to judge me. It's an extraordinary feeling when all at once there's someone in your life who watches you just as you want to be watched. Denis watches me carefully, sympathetically. When he looks at me like that I feel that I no longer have the right to die. There are too many things I have to help him understand. His mother, for one.

Paradoxical as it may seem, the outcome is that I feel both responsible and happy. More cheerful and more carefree. Before Denis was born, I used to make a lot of fuss about little things. Now I have only one thing to worry about. It's very serious, but it does simplify things.

How are you bringing him up?

A child has to have very definite points of reference: his room, his toys, the school he goes to, the people he lives with and the friends he plays with. He shouldn't see anything of his parents' private lives. If he comes home from school with bad marks, you should pull his ears or slap his fingers. But above all, a child needs love and warmth. Warmth and a sense of security.

I refuse to let the papers print photos of him fussing around me. I won't have that. He has a sense of his personal dignity and I don't see why I should take that away from him. My son will never be the son of a famous woman.

Is he the most important person in your life?

The love I feel for my son is the most precious thing in my life. But something dreadful could happen and he wouldn't stop me being unhappy. If I fell in love with someone, who didn't love me or if a friend died, I wouldn't hold back my tears because my son was there. Only a monster can love only her children. And I'm no monster. Merely because I have a son doesn't mean that I have to ignore everything and everyone else.

Does having him mean that you are no longer alone?

When I had my car crash I learned that you are always alone. When you're badly hurt, you're alone. No one can do a thing for you, not even the people who love you. The crash also brought it home to me that you have to be careful, that it's better to be fit than unfit. So much depends upon physical mechanisms. Stupid, silly things like that. Denis can never prevent me from being alone and I can never prevent him from being alone. But we would do anything for each other. We'll be careful.

When I speak of being alone I am referring to solitude, the moral solitude that has become, in my opinion, the other face and the reverse of physical solitude. People tend to have fewer and fewer moments when they feel themselves alone physically. There are fewer and fewer moments when there are no observers to look at them – either kindly or unkindly, it does not matter. (Moreover, I believe that constant sexual promiscuity to avoid loneliness is causing frightening maladjustments.) The only times people are really alone, free to be themselves, is when those around them are looking at television. And I think this is one of the worst aspects revealed by demographic studies. Personally, if I could not be alone one or two hours a day, I would be inclined to feel frightfully alone afterward when I was surrounded by twenty people. In French, there is a difference between "alone" and "solitary"; I do not know if it exists in English.

As to family life, I think it is always possible to achieve it from the instant people have the time to love one another and room in which to express it without bumping into one another or being obsessive. But family life may be life with one's friends or life among centenarians, just as certain lives shared with members of a true family can be a living hell. It depends on the individuals.

Do you have any secrets?

I don't have any secrets. The way to understand a writer is to look for the nostalgia, not the secrets. Secrets are things you hide deliberately. But you cannot hide nostalgia because it is reflected in the books you write.

My moral values are quite simple: respect other people, love them and don't hurt them. I'm passionately interested in literature, music, children, people, the countryside and animals. That's all.

I've gained a few years if nothing else. I've lost the quick reflexes of adolescence. I've gained a few wrinkles, which means I've lost a few patches of skin where once there were no wrinkles. You win some and you lose some.

As you grow older, you learn to know your own limits. You become more supple. You get less annoyed when it's not going well, more confident that you will be able to go on writing. Knowing your limits means that you realize you're not Proust or Dostoevsky. You stop playing with words and trying to impress people with woolly phrases or theories. You learn not to cheat or fool people. You learn not to fool yourself.

If five or six people read my books and feel relieved because they hear a voice that calms them down or gives them a tender or lyrical solution to their problems, it's been worthwhile. Basically I'm a moralist. All writers end up as moralists. You either feel that life is slowing down or that it's going so fast that it's getting out of control. So you try to speed things up or slow them down. And you become a moralist. Besides, I've always been interested in finding an explanation for anxiety, fear and loneliness.

One final word, one last wish.

I wish I were ten again. I wish I weren't an adult.

Bibliography

The following works by Françoise Sagan are available in English translations.

Bonjour Tristesse. John Murray, 1954; Penguin, 1958.

Those Without Shadows. John Murray, 1957; Penguin, 1961.

Aimez-Vous Brahms? John Murray, 1960; Penguin, 1962.

A Certain Smile. John Murray, 1956; Penguin, 1960.

Wonderful Clouds. John Murray, 1961; Penguin, 1965.

La Chamade. John Murray, 1966; Penguin, 1968.

The Heartkeeper. John Murray, 1968; Penguin, 1972.

Sunlight on Cold Water. Weidenfeld and Nicolson, 1971; Penguin, 1973.

Scars on the Soul. André Deutsch, 1974; Penguin, 1977.

Lost Profile. André Deutsch, 1976; Penguin, 1978.

Silken Eyes. André Deutsch, 1977.

The Unmade Bed. Aidan Ellis, 1978.

Notes

1. *Maréchal nous voilà* ... A song in praise of Marshal Petain, sung in French schools under the Vichy government. Translated literally, the title means, "Marshal, savior of the fatherland, we stand before you."

2. The usual punishment administered to women who had associated with German soldiers during the occupation.

3. *Le Sabbat*, The autobiography of Maurice Sachs (1906–1944). Written in 1942, the book gives an account of the artistic life of the interwar period and includes portraits of many of the writers of the time. An English translation was published by Arthur Baker (London) in 1953 under the title, *Day of Wrath. Confessions of a Turbulent Youth.*

4. *La Robe Mauve de Valentine*, Sagan's third play, written and produced in 1963.

5. Crevel, an associate of Breton and the Surrealists, who committed suicide in 1935.

6. *Manifeste des 121*. In late 1960, a group of 121 writers and intellectuals signed a manifesto denouncing French policy in Algeria and calling for active support for the Algerian National Liberation Front.

7. Djamila Boupacha. An Algerian girl tortured by French paratroopers.

8. OAS *Organisation Armée Secrète,* a right-wing terrorist organization opposed to French withdrawal from Algeria and responsible for various outrages in France, including attempts on de Gaulle's life.

9. The abortion manifesto. In 1971, 343 prominent women signed a manifesto proclaiming that they had had illegal abortions and defying the government to prosecute them.